QUILTER'S ACADEMY

Vol. 2—Sophomore Year

A Skill-Building Course in Quiltmaking

Harriet Hargrave & Carrie Hargrave

C&T PUBLISHING

Text and photography copyright © 2010 by Harriet Hargrave and Carrie Hargrave

Artwork copyright © 2010 by C&T Publishing, Inc.

Publisher: Amy Marson

Creative Director: Gailen Runge

Acquisitions Editor: Susanne Woods

Editor: Carrie Hargrave

Copyeditor/Proofreader: Wordfirm Inc.

Book Design Director: Kristen Yenche

Cover/Book Designer: Kerry Graham

Page Layout Artist: Publishers' Design and Production Services, Inc.

Production Coordinator: Zinnia Heinzmann

Production Editor: Alice Mace Nakanishi

Illustrator: Aliza Shalit

Photography by Brian Birlauf, unless otherwise noted

Published by C&T Publishing, Inc., P.O. Box 1456, Lafayette, CA 94549

Library of Congress Cataloging-in-Publication Data

Hargrave, Harriet.

Quilter's Academy Vol 1.- Freshman Year : a skill-building course in quiltmaking / by Harriet Hargrave and Carrie Hargrave.

p. cm.

ISBN 978-1-57120-594-0 (softcover)

1. Patchwork. 2. Quilting. I. Hargrave, Carrie, 1976- II. Title.

TT835.H3384 2009

746.46--dc22

2009008787

Printed in China

10 9 8 7 6 5 4 3 2 1

A Course in Quilting

A fresh new approach to uncovering the details that make quilting fun and rewarding for the beginner.

Quilting 201—Sophomore Year

Continuing with strips and squares, but now jazzing them up by putting them on-point in a diagonal set, adding sashing and window-paning, and working in wonderful pieced frames and borders to continue your journey into quiltmaking skills.

Dedication

We would like to dedicate this book to Mary Ellen Hopkins, who has been a tremendous influence on both of us. Mary Ellen brought machine piecing to the forefront in the early 1980s. She made it okay for us to get our quilt tops done quickly and have fun doing it. Creativity and free thinking were her strong points. The borders that are designed through the diagonal-set piecing in this book were the brainchild of Mary Ellen. She called them Incorporated Borders, meaning they are designed using a block on-point to create the piecing of a straight-appearing border. They have also been called Painless Borders by Sally Schneider, but they originated in a Summer Camp seminar with Mary Ellen.

Harriet participated in Mary Ellen's *It's Okay if You Sit on My Quilt* seminars for several years before she started to teach at them with Mary Ellen throughout the 1980s. Carrie met Mary Ellen when she was a young girl and had her impression of quilters changed forever. There is never a better time to be had by all than in the presence of Mary Ellen. Her methods and designs have influenced both of us for years. Thank you for the fun and inspiration!

Last, but certainly not least, to all the thousands of Harriet's students who have influenced her desire to be the very best teacher she could be during the past 32 years. We hope that the passion runs as deep in them as it does in us.

The authors take full responsibility for the contents of this book, including the technical accuracy of the information. Please direct any questions to quilt.academy.q.a@earthlink.net or visit the authors' blog at http://quiltersacademy.blogspot.com.

Contents

Preface

You are holding the second in a series of six books. The purpose of the series is to build your quiltmaking skills on a firm foundation from beginner to advanced. Volume 1 laid the foundation for all the rest of the books. If you have not worked through Volume 1 entirely, we *strongly* suggest that you do so first. These books are not all-inclusive. This second volume is to be used as a workbook. It contains a complete sequence of classes, lessons, exercises, and projects that will build your skills from one project to the next. We highly recommend that you make the quilts in the order presented, as we have placed them in order of complexity. Each quilt offers new challenges and techniques that will help you continually build your skill level. We have chosen designs that are timeless and very adaptable to traditional fabrics, as well as to more upbeat fabric and color choices. Use these quilts to explore your color and style preferences.

This volume and the first in the series deal with quilts made up of strips and squares. By mastering the techniques in these first two books, you are laying a foundation for precise, high-quality piecing. There are hundreds of quilts based on strips and squares, so you can spend a long time exploring these stunning quilts before you jump into the more complex piecing in the following books.

Introduction

We hope you are as excited about what is in this book—your sophomore year—as we are. We had a great time coming up with the quilts, and especially developing the designing tools in Class 250. We have tried to make it easy for you to develop your own ideas with worksheets, graph paper, and drop-in linking blocks. You will find it amazing how many awesome quilts you can make while still working with strips and squares, but changing the setting and design elements.

This book takes you from basic, fairly easy quilts to more and more complex designs. As you progress through the classes, the actual how-to instructions for each quilt will become less detailed. We are confident that your skills are getting to where you do not need as much hand-holding as you progress. The skills are building on themselves, and the basic sewing methods repeat over and over. If you have not gone through *Quilter's Academy Volume 1,* we strongly suggest that you do so before moving on to this book. You are likely to find some areas where you might not understand what is going on if you haven't been building your skills with us from the beginning. This is truly a "college course" in quiltmaking, not a pattern book.

Volume 3 will take you into the infinite design options of triangles. The fun just continues! Happy quilting!

—Harriet and Carrie

Class 210

In Volume 1, we discussed the very minimum workspace needed for learning the basics. This Class expands on the basics to help you set up an even more efficient workspace. We discuss upgrading your space and equipment as you get further into piecing and as the quilt tops get larger. If sewing is new to you, you will enjoy learning more about your sewing machine, including tension basics, proper needle selection, and basic maintenance. We cover the basics of thread selection, including the meaning of various sizes, weights, and plies and the appropriate use of each. We also discuss specialty rulers that make the process of measuring diagonal setting triangles easier and more efficient.

how to use this book

This is the second volume in a series of six. If you are just discovering this book and haven't yet worked through Volume 1, we strongly suggest that you do so first. Volume 1 covers in detail all the basics of straightening fabric grain, cutting successfully, working with rulers, sewing accurate seams for exact results, and pressing and ironing properly. Volume 2 only reviews some of these processes, as there is no reason to rewrite Volume 1 in every subsequent volume. If you don't understand all the techniques in this volume, refer to Volume 1, as we have tried very hard to follow through from book to book for consistency. Like Volume 1, this book will build your skills class by class, lesson by lesson. We don't recommend that you jump in just anywhere and make a project because you like the quilt photo. The projects are stepping stones, leading from one skill to another, increasing in difficulty as you go.

LESSON ONE:

Expanding your sewing area

Now that you have made a few quilt tops, you are probably wishing for a little more workspace. If in Volume 1 you worked on a dining room table, you no doubt found that the larger quilt tops would drop off the area surrounding your machine and catch on its edges. The most rewarding way to work is at a machine that is dropped into a table or cabinet so that the machine bed is level with the tabletop. The tabletop surface must be large enough to support the entire size of your project.

SEWING MACHINE AREA

If you are starting to develop a sewing area, but either don't have the dedicated space or are unable to afford a cabinet, Safco offers a wonderful table that is inexpensive and portable, but larger than the table discussed in Volume 1.

Safco computer table used as a sewing cabinet

This folding compact computer table is a perfect height for sewing (it measures 47½″ wide × 29¾″ deep × 28¾″ high). The table includes a six-position drop-down tray that is 20¾″ × 9½″ (where a computer keyboard usually sits) upon which you can place your sewing machine. The tabletop is ¾″ laminate, providing strength and durability. With a bit of ingenuity, you can create a surround for the opening and develop a flat-bed system for the machine—just like a sewing cabinet, but at a fraction of the price.

You could also adapt the Sew Steady Junior table featured in Volume 1. If your machine came with a sewing table that attaches to it, use that as your insert to fill in the area.

Larger furniture means you will need an entire corner or part of a room to set up a small sewing area. Carrie has turned an area of her basement into a very efficient workspace. A Safco table, a Big Board, and filing cabinets meet most of her basic piecing needs.

Carrie's sewing area

IRONING AREA

Another wonderful addition to your equipment is a Big Board ironing board, which is more than worth the investment. The Big Board is a sheet of ½″–⅝″-thick hardwood that measures 22″ × 60″. The frame on the bottom side of the board fits on top of a standard ironing board. This very large, flat, hard surface is the perfect place to work with a quilt top.

If you cannot get an actual Big Board, you can make something similar. Cut a high-quality sheet of plywood to the width and length you want. Add rails to the bottom the width of your ironing board, as well as an end to fit up against the end of the ironing board to keep the large board from sliding. Cover the wood with an old army blanket or ⅛″-thick cotton batting, and then cover this with pillow ticking or a heavy cotton fabric. Now you have an ironing surface that will serve you well for years. This board can be fit to your ironing board or placed on top of a table. Some quilters have an ironing surface that fits the

top of their cutting table for an extra-large pressing area. If you have limited space, you could adhere large cutting mats to one side of the board, using that side for cutting and then flipping the board for pressing.

Big Board

Once you get used to a very hard, flat, firm surface, you will never go back to a small, squishy ironing board. It even makes ironing clothes faster and easier, as the entire back of a shirt fits on the board at once! Make sure you do not use the silver Teflon ironing board covers, however, as they are too slick for the control needed when pressing seams in piecing, and they do not allow your fabric to dry when you use steam or starch.

LESSON TWO:
Sewing machines

If you are new to sewing, you may be a bit intimidated by your sewing machine. When it acts up (which they do quite often), you may not have any idea what to do to keep it going. This lesson covers the most basic things you need to know and understand about sewing machines:

❋ Basic cleaning and oiling

❋ Tension system

❋ Needle sizes and types for various uses

HELP! MY MACHINE IS ACTING UP!

You are sewing along, and all of a sudden the stitches look terrible, or the thread jams, or the machine starts to sound different. What is going on? When any of these issues occurs, follow these steps to try to get your machine back on track:

❀ Stop sewing and take all the thread out of the machine, both the top and the bobbin. Check the bobbin area for loose threads or lint. If the machine is very linty, you will need to blow it out (this will be discussed later in the Class, page 8). Carefully rethread the machine top and bottom, and then try sewing again.

❀ If the problem persists, change the needle. Make sure that you have the correct size needle for the fabric and thread you are using (see page 12 for more on this topic).

These two steps usually take care of most of the basic sewing problems encountered in quilting. Read on for details about these issues.

BASIC MACHINE MAINTENANCE

Before starting a new project, be sure to clean and oil your machine. A well-maintained machine will give you many hours of sewing pleasure.

❀ *Thoroughly clean the bobbin area with a lint brush.* Often the smallest amount of lint or debris can cause the machine to skip stitches and have tension problems. Use brushes, cotton swabs, or pipe cleaners to remove lint from every reachable area. Tweezers can be used to remove caught threads, but otherwise avoid using metal tools for cleaning, as they can create burrs that can lead to thread breakage.

Cleaning bobbin area of machine (front case)

Cleaning bobbin area of machine (drop-in)

Cleaning under drop-in housing

❀ *Remove the throat plate cover that is around the feed dogs.* Brush out the lint between the feed dogs. Scrub the feed dogs with a toothbrush. Use a small vacuum attachment meant for computers to suck away loose particles. Then use a blower or canned air to blow out the tiny particles not removed by suction.

Cleaning feed dogs

✻ *Canned air is an excellent tool for getting rid of lint* from the crevices in the bobbin and feed dog area, but take caution when using it. The accelerant creates a very cold stream of air. Make sure to aim the nozzle at least 2″ away from the metal parts. This allows the air to warm a bit. If you don't, the air can condense on the metal, which over time can pit the metal. In addition, work from the back of the machine and blow any debris out toward the front. If you point the nozzle into the area, lint will move down into the arm of the machine, where you will be unable to reach to remove it.

Using canned air from back of machine

✻ *Check the machine's tension disks for any lint or residue.* Clean between the tension disks with a pipe cleaner. If you tend to use polyester or low-quality thread, adding a little lighter fluid or rubbing alcohol (just damp) to the pipe cleaner will dissolve any residue left by the thread finish on the tension disks.

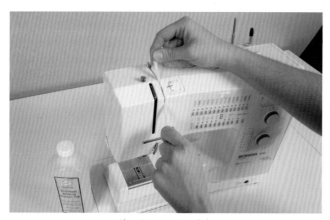

Cleaning tension disks

✻ *Check the tension clip on the bobbin case* (the clip that the thread goes under when you thread the bobbin case). This clip may contain lint or pieces of thread that can cause the tension to vary, and cause poor stitches. Run a piece of heavier thread under the clip, as though using dental floss, to dislodge any lint or threads. Clean the inside of the bobbin case, as lint buildup can cause the bobbin to spin unevenly, which can also affect stitch quality.

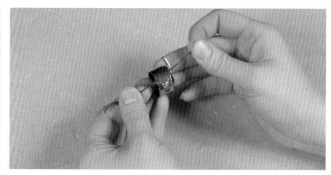

Cleaning bobbin tension clip

✻ *Lightly oil the shuttle and race of the bobbin area every time you clean it.* Use only high-quality synthetic oil that has no detergents (this oil can be purchased from your sewing machine dealer). Regular petroleum or household oils will eventually cause the mechanisms to lock up. Do not spray silicone or products such as WD-40 into the machine; these products tend to overspray, and many parts of your machine need to remain completely free of lubricant. Be sure to check with your sewing machine mechanic for specifics relating to your particular machine.

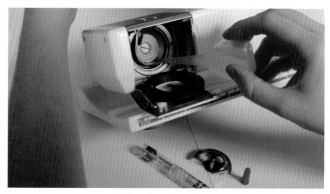

Oiling shuttle and race

✻ *Once a month, if you're sewing a great deal or doing a lot of quilting, put a drop of sewing machine oil on the needle bar* (take the needle out before oiling). Let the machine run for a minute or two after applying the oil, then let it sit for a few minutes so the excess oil can drain off. When not sewing, lower the needle into soft cotton fabric so that any excess oil can wick into the fabric.

Oiling the needle bar

❋ *Clean the body of the machine and wax it with a high-quality car wax made for enameled steel parts or with a wax for plastic-body machines. Keep the machine covered when not in use to prevent accumulation of dust and dirt particles.*

After you've cleaned and oiled the machine, it is time to put in a new needle that is appropriate for the sewing technique you'll be doing. Check your manual to see if the flat side of the needle goes to the back or to the side if you are unsure. When inserting the needle, push it up until it hits the stop, and then tighten the screw. Do not apply too much pressure on the needle clamp screw, as you can easily break off the point that holds the needle in place. Tighten until firm. If the needle is not inserted properly, the machine will skip stitches, if it will stitch at all. When sewing, listen to the sound of your machine. Any time you hear a punching sound, stop and change the needle. A dull or bent needle can damage the machine.

TENSIONS

> *tip* Read through the entire section on tension before making any changes to your machine. At the end of this unit you will find suggestions for making samples to test the machine before you start each new project or change to a different thread.

Once the machine is cleaned and oiled and the appropriate needle is properly in place, it's time to adjust the tension for a perfect stitch. Minor tension adjustments might be needed when changing to different fabrics and/or different threads. Before you start a new project, test your machine by stitching a sample of the new material or thread. Inspect the stitch tension, and make the appropriate adjustments. Read on to learn how.

Understanding top tension

When doing any type of machine work, make yourself comfortable with the tension adjustments necessary for the machine to properly stitch different threads and fabric weights. There is no magic about thread tension; with a thorough understanding of your machine's tension system, you can eliminate many service calls.

When getting to know your machine, you'll find it necessary to have a full understanding of its tension system. To begin, identify the top-tension adjustment dial on your machine.

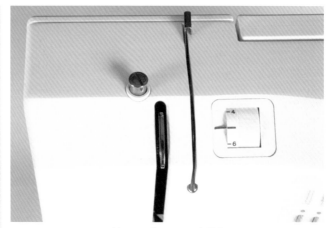

Top-tension control dial

Top-tension control on front of machine

Many of the newer computerized machines have an internal tension system. You will need to get into the tension screen or program and learn to adjust the top tension through the computer. Be sure to read your manual, as each computer system can be very different.

The following exercise will help you learn about tension adjustment. Begin by threading the top of the machine with a 50/3 or 60/3 cotton sewing thread. *Always be sure the presser foot is in the up position when threading.* Do not thread the needle. Lower the presser foot to engage the tension. Position the top-thread dial at "normal" for your machine and start to pull the thread through the machine. As you pull the thread, lower the tension dial to a lower number, one number at a time. You should notice the thread getting looser and easier to pull as the numbers get smaller. When you get to zero, there should be no drag on the thread.

The lower the number, the looser the tension.

Now go back to the "normal" setting. Pull the thread through again, this time moving the dial up to the higher numbers. The thread will get tighter and harder to pull. When you get to nine or ten, the thread won't budge.

The higher the number, the tighter the tension.

UNDERSTANDING BOBBIN TENSION

To learn about bobbin tension, wind a bobbin with 50- or 60-weight three-ply mercerized cotton sewing thread. Do not use polyester or cotton-covered polyester to test bobbin tension for quilting.

Begin the winding process by putting the tail end of the thread through the hole in the side of the bobbin, if your bobbin has one. Hold this end tightly until the thread has wrapped a couple of times up and down in the bobbin. Then snip off the thread so it is even with the bobbin. Never let the thread wrap over the edge of the bobbin, as this can cause the bobbin to feed unevenly.

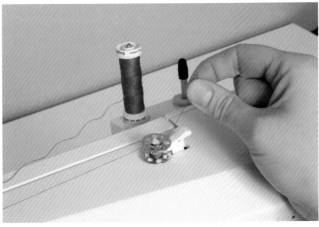

Holding thread to wind a bobbin

Be sure you have the correct bobbins for your model and brand of machine. Purchase your bobbins only from your dealer and make sure they are exactly like the ones that originally came with your machine.

Tension can be affected by how the bobbin is wound. When winding the bobbin, make sure that it is winding smoothly and evenly and that the thread is being wound tight. Loose, unevenly wound bobbins cause poor stitch quality. Also, always start with an empty bobbin. You do not want to wind a new thread on top of a thread already wound on a bobbin. This can cause your bobbin to be unbalanced and the new thread to not wind as evenly and tightly as it would if it were wound on an empty bobbin.

Poorly wound bobbins compared to a properly wound bobbin

> *tip*
>
> If you have specialty thread wound on a bobbin and don't want to confuse it with other threads, insert a pipe cleaner through the center of the bobbin and the corresponding spool of thread; then tie the ends of the pipe cleaner together. These thread/bobbin marriages are a great way to identify and store specialty threads such as jeans or washaway thread or even bobbins that match a specific color of your sewing thread.

When placing the bobbin in the bobbin case, make sure that it unwinds according to your manual. On machines with an actual bobbin case that loads in the front, the bobbins usually unwind clockwise when you look at the bobbin in the case. However, a few unwind counterclockwise, so be sure to check your machine's manual. If you have a drop-in bobbin system, find out whether the bobbin spins clockwise or counterclockwise. In addition, be certain that you have secured the thread under the tension clip. Finally, be sure to thread the top of the machine with the same thread used to wind the bobbin. These seemingly small items have a big impact on stitch quality.

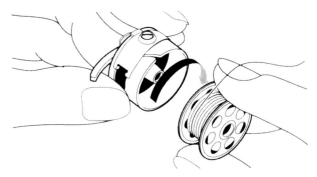

Correct threading of bobbin

If you need to adjust the bobbin tension, be sure to make a note of exactly what you do. Keep a pad of self-stick notes by your machine to record whatever adjustments you make. First, draw the clock face diagram as shown below on a note. Then, hold the bobbin case exactly as shown (bobbin on the left, bobbin case upright). Before you make any adjustments, indicate on your drawing where the screwhead is positioned.

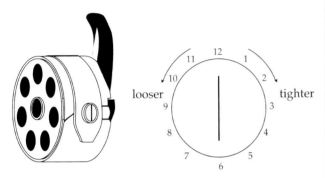

Using "clock face" as a guide for adjusting tension

If you have a drop-in bobbin housing, you will need to learn how to remove this unit for adjustments and cleaning, just like a bobbin case. All drop-in housings have a small screw on the side, and the adjustment is the same as for a regular bobbin case. Read the screwhead from the same angle as it sits in the machine. Some machines actually have markings on the housing so you can easily adjust the tension. Because every brand is a bit different, you will have to work this out with the help of your manual or your mechanic.

Drop-in bobbin housings

On either type of bobbin system, the screw and the notation on the paper are the same. Before you adjust the bobbin case, remember to make notes as you go. To make an adjustment, turn the tension screw on the tension clip.

Turn it to the right to tighten and to the left to loosen—remember the old saying, "Righty tighty, lefty loosey." Look at the screw as if it were a hand on a clock. Adjust the screw in one-hour (or five-minute) increments. Continue to adjust this screw in very small increments until the tension is correct. Make a new stitched sample after each adjustment. Compare each of your sewn samples with the following illustrations. You want your stitches to lock between the two fabrics, not on the top or bottom of the fabric surface.

Once you have the correct adjustment, draw a new line on your note, indicating the new position of the screw. Then make a notation to remind yourself where the screw started and that you turned it to the right (or to the left) to the new "time." When you are finished working with that combination of thread and fabric, you can read the note and know exactly how far back to the left (or the right) to turn the screw. Nothing has been harmed, and the machine is ready to test for your next project.

Adjusting the tension is not a huge problem with most common threads and fabrics. We cover it here so that when you do have a problem, you will know how to deal with it.

CHECKING FOR PROPER TENSION

Now let's make a sample to see how the machine is going to sew with the "normal," or preset, tension settings. Using the threads that you used above, carefully thread the machine top and bobbin. Use an 80/12 needle for 50/3 thread or a 75/11 needle for 60/3 thread. Sew a row of stitches in two layers of fabric. You will know the tension is correct when both threads are linked in the center of the two layers of fabric, as shown.

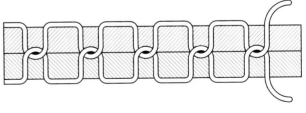

Balanced tension

The next illustration shows the bottom thread being pulled too tight, indicating that the top thread is too loose or the bobbin thread is too tight.

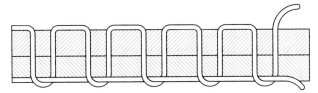

Top tension too loose or bobbin too tight

The next illustration shows the top thread being pulled too tight, which can indicate that the top thread is too tight or the bobbin thread is too loose.

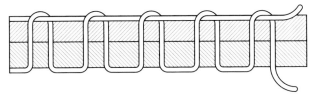

Top tension too tight or bobbin too loose

Once you've made a sample of the stitching and determined whether changes need to be made, always start by adjusting the top tension first. Many stitch problems can be corrected simply by loosening the top tension. Adjust by one-half number at a time; never make severe adjustments. If the top tension is too loose, you will see loops of thread forming on the bottom of the fabric. If the problem isn't resolved by adjusting the top tension only, then adjust the bobbin tension, seeking a balance to accommodate the thread. Remember, the tension can change, depending on the type and thickness of the fabric as well as on the thread weight and needle size.

---

tip — If you're not happy with the stitch quality, start troubleshooting for possible problems:

Is the needle the proper size for the thread it is carrying?

Is the needle the proper type for your machine brand?

Is the top thread securely in between the tension disks?

Is the bobbin inserted in the case properly?

Is there any lint in the feed dog area?

Do the top and bottom threads match in size and weight?

NEEDLES

The sewing machine needle is probably the number one cause of problems for sewers. It is the first thing to check when you are experiencing stitch problems. High-quality needles are critical to achieving smooth, even stitches. *Use the needle type, size, and brand recommended for your machine.* In addition, use a needle that complements your thread choice. Always start each project with a new needle. We can't stress enough that not only your understanding of needles and thread but also your choices about them will directly affect whether your machine sews to the best of its ability.

PARTS OF A NEEDLE

Examine a large machine needle, such as a 100/16 (see illustration). Notice that the needle is flat on the backside of the shank and has a long thread groove on the opposite side. The flat shank provides perfect positioning of the needle in the needle bar and in relation to the point of the hook. Run your fingernail down the groove. This groove protects the thread within the needle as it penetrates the fabric. The thread slides through the grooved side and the eye. When a stitch is formed, the thread is pinched between the fabric and the needle, creating a loop behind the needle as the needle rises. This loop and the scarf (the hollowed-out area on the back of the needle) allow the hook point of the shuttle to pass between the thread and the needle, locking the stitch.

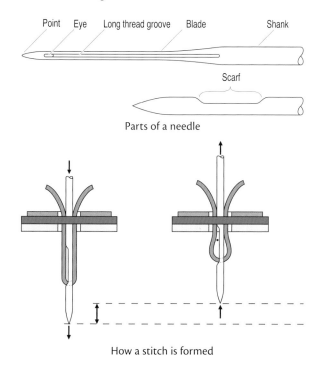

Parts of a needle

How a stitch is formed

NEEDLE **BRANDS**

Schmetz is one of the most recognized needle brands on the market, but it does not fit every machine. Klasse is another commonly found brand that is very similar to Schmetz. If you have a Singer, especially an older one, make sure that you use Singer brand needles. Janome recommends that Organ needles be used in its machines. Different brand needles have a different position for the eye, a different length from the eye to the point, and/or a different scarf on the back of the needle that affects the machine's ability to stitch properly.

Various brands of needles

NEEDLE SIZES AND TYPES

The information that you need in order to choose the correct needle is printed on the front of the needle packet. We are using Schmetz packages as an example. Different letters and numbers may be used on different needle brands; be sure to familiarize yourself with your machine's requirements. Needles sold for industrial machines use a completely different system. On a Schmetz package, under the brand name is the type of needle, referring to the type of point the needle has—universal, topstitching, jeans/denim, microtex, and so forth. Below that is a series of numbers, which refer to the needle shank shape and the length and shape of the needle's point. The first set of numbers refers to the needle system. For example, in 130/705, the "130" refers to the shank length, and the "705" indicates that it is a flat shank. These numbers will help you determine which needle system is suitable for your particular machine.

The first letter after the numbers refers to needle scarf (e.g., H indicates needle scarf, B indicates no needle scarf). The next letter indicates the type of needle point (M = sharp, J = denim, Q = quilting, E = embroidery, and so on). The shank of the needle is also often marked with a color to help you identify the type of point once the needle is removed from the packet.

The needle size is indicated in both metric and U.S. sizes. The metric number represents the needle diameter (size 70/10 = 0.7 mm). This set of numbers will help you determine the needle's suitability for a given fabric, thread size, or sewing process.

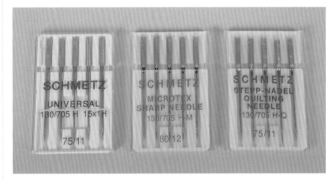

Needle packet information

The universal point needle, which has a slightly rounded point, has long been the standard sewing machine needle. The newer sharp microtex needles were developed to sew silk, microfibers, and other new textiles that require a sharp piercing point to prevent puckered seams. These new needles are also excellent for topstitching, which requires a very straight line of visible stitches. The universal needle performs beautifully for sewing patchwork seams at a much lower cost than the microtex needles, which wear down quickly and must be changed more often than universals. As a beginner, it may be difficult for you to see a difference in the stitch quality of the two different needles. However, try sewing a seam using each needle type to see which you prefer. We recommend that you stick with universals unless you are sewing batik fabrics, which require a microtex needle.

As for size, the needle, thread, and fabric all need to marry together. The needle carries the thread through the fabric; therefore, the hole made by the needle must be large enough to accommodate the thread size. The thread groove should be deep enough to allow the thread to lie in it. The needle eye must also be the right size. If it is too small for the thread to pass through, the thread will fray and break, and stitches will be skipped. If the thread is too fine for the needle, the hole made by the needle will not be filled by the thread, resulting in a weak and unsightly seam. The more room the thread has to flop around in the eye, the harder it is on the thread.

The chart below gives corresponding needle and thread sizes to assist you in choosing a needle for the thread size and fabric weight you are sewing. As a general guide, start with the smallest needle size recommended for your thread weight and ply. If the thread breaks or skips stitches, go to the next larger size.

Needle/Thread Reference

Thread Size	Needle Size							
	60	65	70	75	80	90	100	110
Ultra fine thread 80/2	I	I						
Nylon monofilament thread		I	I	I	I			
Fine machine embroidery thread 60/2			I	I	I			
Machine embroidery thread 50/2		I	I	I				
Embroidery thread 30/2				I	I	I		
Merc. cotton sewing thread 60/3				I	I			
Merc. cotton sewing thread 50/3					I	I		
Synthetic sewing thread (spun)					I	I		
Cotton-wrapped polyester thread							I	
Cotton hand quilting thread							I	I
Buttonhole (cordonnet) thread							I	I

Threads

Right up front, we will state that you need to use only 100 percent cotton thread when piecing. When polyester fabrics were introduced years ago, polyester threads were needed for strength and stretchability. This thread overtook the market, and 100 percent cotton thread was difficult to obtain. Once quilting took off in the 1980s, however, cotton thread became king again. We are now facing the polyester problem anew, as some thread companies are trying to push polyester on us again—to the serious detriment of our quilts in the years ahead. Consider these facts:

❋ Threads and fabrics need to be of like fibers—for example, natural-fiber fabrics should be sewn with natural-fiber threads.

❋ The thread should be weaker than the fabric. Thread that is too strong will cut and weaken the fabric in the seam, causing the fabric to "break." If a thread breaks in a seam, the seam can be mended; if the fabric tears, it cannot be mended.

❋ Thread size should be as fine as possible, but it should always be consistent with the strength requirement of the seam. Finer threads tend to become buried below the surface of the fabric and are subjected to less abrasion than seams with heavier thread, which are on top of the fabric. Finer threads also require smaller needles, producing less fabric distortion than heavier needles do.

WARNING

When piecing, do not buy 50/2 or 60/2 threads, such as Aurifil, DMC, or Mettler Fine Embroidery thread. These are machine embroidery threads and are too weak for the stresses of pieced seams. These threads are good for paper piecing with a shortened stitch length, for appliqué, for machine embroidery, and for very close machine quilting.

The preferred thread size for sewing cotton quilting fabric has always been 50/3. The "50" designates the yarn count of the thread, or its weight and diameter. The "3" indicates the number of plies twisted together. The higher the first number, the finer the thread. The more plies, the stronger the thread. A new thread has recently been introduced: 60/3. This thread is finer than the 50 but is almost as strong because of the three plies. Because it is finer, a smaller needle can be used, giving nicer-quality stitches. It also accommodates the ¼" seam allowance better, as it takes up less space in the seam.

---

the slide test

Here is Carrie's great way for testing whether your thread fits the eye of your needle: Thread a machine needle with a length of thread. Hold the thread in front of you horizontally. Tip one end of the thread at a 45° angle. If the needle doesn't move, the eye is too small; try a larger needle. If the needle flies down the thread, the eye is too large; try a smaller needle. If the needle skips easily down the thread, you have found the needle size to stitch with; just double-check for stitch quality.

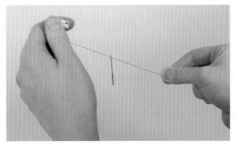

Testing needle size

Thread strength should be less than that of the fabric to be sewn. Authorities agree that the seam strength should be about 60–70 percent of the fabric strength. The reason for this is if excessive stress is placed on a seam, the thread in the seam will break instead of the fabric. Cotton thread is weaker than cotton fabric; polyester thread is not. In addition, polyester thread has tiny, abrasive edges that work as saw blades against the soft cotton fibers, and cut through the seams over time.

When purchasing cotton threads, unroll a length and check for quality. A fuzzy thread is made from short fibers, rendering it weak and giving it poor sewing properties. Finding uneven areas, called slubs, is another indication of a lower-quality thread. A thread with very few or no fuzzy ends is generally made from long fibers. This thread will sew a nicer seam and will last longer in the finished seam.

LESSON FOUR:
More rulers

As you progress into more and more techniques, you will be adding specialty rulers to your collection.

Diagonal-set quilt tops take a bit more measuring and preparation before borders can be added, and a long see-through ruler can be really helpful. Creative Grids has a 36½" × 2½" yardstick-type ruler in see-through acrylic. This length is very useful for measuring along the side of a quilt top to align markings with a long, straight edge.

There are also rulers for measuring the side-setting triangles of diagonal sets. If you have a real aversion to formulas and math, you'll find these rulers to be a great help, as they take the math out of the process. You won't need to do the calculations or remember the formulas with these specialty rulers. In addition, they work with strips instead of squares. These techniques will be covered in detail in Class 230, Lesson 2 (page 23).

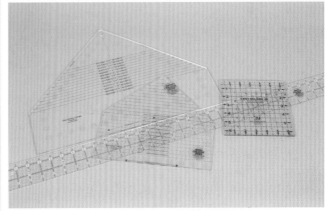

Rulers for diagonal sets

Class 220

Why cotton fabric?

If you are a new quilter, you are no doubt confused by the dos and don'ts of caring for fabrics. If you've been quilting for a while, you might find that you want a change in the finished look of the quilts you're making now as compared to those you made in the past. Your style and tastes will most likely continue to change over time. Wherever you are in your quilting journey, you will need to know how to treat your fabrics based on your preferences, needs, and desires.

> *hint* The information in this Class is a condensed form of the valuable information available in Harriet's book *From Fiber to Fabric*. This is a textile book for quiltmakers who really want to understand the products they are working with—fabric, thread, and batting. Her book is now available as an e-book from C&T Publishing (see Resources, page 112).

WHY DO QUILTERS PREFER COTTON TO BLENDS?

Careful consideration of fiber content in the fabrics you choose can affect not only your success in piecing a quilt top but also the durability of the finished quilt. The fiber of choice for quiltmakers is 100 percent cotton. Between the 1950s and the 1970s, polyester was the predominant fiber. It was next to impossible to purchase 100 percent cotton, and when you did find it, the selection was very limited. When quiltmaking was revived in the mid-1970s, the demand for cotton fabric began to grow. The new generation of quiltmakers soon learned what the longtime quilters already knew: cotton is superior to polyester and cotton/polyester blends when piecing, appliquéing, and quilting.

Today, quilters enjoy choosing from thousands of beautiful 100 percent cotton fabrics, printed in every color, style, and trend imaginable. The following list explains the benefits of using cotton in quilts, as opposed to using synthetic fibers.

❋ **Cotton can retain its pressed form,** giving a sharp crispness to a pressed seam or an appliquéd edge. Cotton's flexibility allows you to work any little puckers out of a seam allowance with a good pressing. The seams in cotton fabrics will lie flat, which is a necessity for accurate piecing and machine quilting.

❋ **Polyester blends are made to release wrinkles.** They naturally resist the knife-edge press needed for flat seam allowances, causing the seams to lift.

❋ **Distortion is minimal** when only 100 percent cottons are used in patchwork.

❋ **Sewing cottons and polyester blends together can result in mismatched seams with puffy seam allowances,** no matter how carefully you sew. If you have to combine different fabrics, stay clear of "wobbly," low-thread-count fabrics and stretchy or slick fabrics. Try to make certain that the fabric weights are compatible. A heavier, coarser fabric will weaken the lighter fabric to which it's stitched, causing the seam to wear out.

❋ **Cotton is more opaque than polyester,** which reduces the problem of seam allowances showing through the quilt's top layer.

❋ **Batting bearding is less prevalent in 100 percent cottons** than in blends. Static electricity, as well as a low thread count of the fabric, can cause the batting fibers to work through to the fabric's surface. Because of the lack of static in cotton, this problem is less prevalent than with polyester.

❋ **Cotton is easy to quilt** because of the soft cotton yarns used to weave the fabric. The exception is batik fabrics, which have tightly twisted yarns used in the weaving, a high thread count, and a hard finish. We recommend that you stay away from batiks until you have your basic skills mastered.

❋ **Cotton sticks to itself** and prevents slipping while you are piecing small pieces together.

❋ **Cottons will tear on-grain,** making it possible to find the true crosswise grain so that straightening is accurate.

STANDARDS AND EXPECTATIONS

Not all cotton fabrics are created equally. Price very often reflects quality. However, a higher price alone does not always signify a trouble-free fabric! When choosing fabrics for quiltmaking, you must take into consideration thread count, shrinkage, lightfastness, crocking, and colorfastness to washing.

❋ **Are there actually different qualities of the same print?** We all must become informed, conscientious consumers. Today, there are many manufacturers producing beautiful, top-quality fabrics for quiltmaking. Considering the price at which these fabrics are sold, we are extremely fortunate to have them available. The industry does, however, make different grades of fabrics for various end uses. If you do not know about the different qualities and how to tell them apart, you will likely purchase some products that are not appropriate for quiltmaking.

You might also see the same prints in various retail establishments at substantially different prices. Be aware that the print can be on different qualities of cloth (greige goods) and that the quality of the dye and/or finish can also differ. Price is often a good indication of the quality discrepancy.

It doesn't make sense to work with inferior products, and it need not happen. You just need to take the time to learn about fabric testing. And don't assume that brands found only in quilt shops are always the highest quality. It is becoming common for many well-respected and recognized brand names to change the thread count or the finish quality to try to save on manufacturing costs. Once you learn to look beyond the color, pattern, and print, you will notice the quality and know whether it justifies the price.

❋ **Thread count** is one way to determine how many years a fabric can last, what chance the batting will have of coming through the fabric, what percentage of shrinkage there will be, and how high the print quality will be. Be aware that thread count (and dye and finish quality) can fluctuate within a brand, within a season, and between different types of retailers. Try not to depend on brand or price for quality and consistency. Thread count is not stated on the bolt board. Quilting cottons are woven as an even-weave fabric, meaning that both the filling (crosswise grain) and warp (lengthwise grain) have the same number of yarns.

For the past few years, cottons targeted for the quilting market have been woven at 68 threads per square inch. However, we have found that more and more companies are cutting corners and going to 60 threads per square inch. You will find that this lower thread count does not give as clear a print as the higher thread count, and the hand or feel is more coarse. You can truly tell the difference in these higher and lower thread counts when you try to sew them all together in one project.

❋ **Did you know that cotton fibers themselves are relatively stable and do not stretch or shrink?** Shrinkage is one of a quilter's biggest concerns, and thus many quilters automatically prewash their fabrics. This fear of shrinkage is directly related to dressmaking experiences. In garment making, large units of fabric with various grainlines are sewn together. There is no added stability to the fabric other than the seams. When washed, the residual shrinkage of the large pieces of cloth can be noticeable. In quiltmaking, however, we cut small pieces and sew them to other fabrics, stabilizing all edges. Then we layer these joined pieces onto a batting and backing, stitching through all the layers. No one small piece of fabric will shrink more than the batting or backing. In fact, the batting is the strongest determinant of shrinkage in a quilt, not the individual fabrics in the piecing.

❋ **Tumble dryers and dryer heat are large contributors to shrinkage in natural fibers.** Most shrinkage occurs when drying the last 25 percent of moisture out of the fabric. Dryer temperatures should never exceed 160°F (140°F is best). Consider drying cottons on a low setting and removing them from the dryer when they are still slightly damp. Air and line drying are two ways to avoid possible problems the dryer might cause.

LESSON TWO:
Colorfast issues

Colorfastness technically refers to a color's permanence, or its ability to remain unchanged throughout the useful life of the article to which it has been applied.

As you begin to choose fabric colors for your projects, be aware that some colors are more prone to problems than others. *Colorfastness* is a word that is used generically, but there are different types of colorfast issues that fabric can exhibit.

There are many aspects to colorfast issues with cotton fabric. It is not just bleeding in water. Each aspect needs to be considered for each type of quilt you make. For example, if the quilt is going to hang on a wall in a very bright room with many windows or lie on a bed as a bedspread near a window, lightfastness needs to be considered. If the quilt is for a baby and will be laundered all the time, washfastness is of concern. If the quilt will be on a sofa or bed and be romped on and sat on frequently, crocking can be a problem. These concerns are discussed in more detail below.

Not all fabrics have problems with all of these issues. Some colors can withstand washing but will fade readily in direct light. Other colors are very sensitive to chlorine in water but will seldom fade when exposed to light.

The fabrics that can be the most problematic are batiks and any fabrics in rich, dark jewel tones. Any color that contains a high percentage of red may cause trouble. Purples, dark browns, dark greens, maroons, reds, and navy blues *might* also be a problem. In contrast, pastels, lights, and medium prints are generally free of many problems.

❋ *Lightfastness* is the ability of a fabric to stand up to light. Dyed fabrics that are exposed to light can, in time, fade or change color. Both natural sunlight and artificial light can damage color. This damage depends on the intensity of the light source and the amount of exposure, as well as the properties of the dyestuff. Serious consideration must be made when choosing fabrics for bed covers and wall quilts that will be exposed to light for long periods of time.

❋ *Crocking* is the transference of color from abrasion, or the transference of color from rubbing one colored fabric against another. Dark colors are more likely to crock than are light colors. Printed fabrics tend to crock more easily than dyed fabrics, because most of the coloring agent of printed fabric is on the surface and not inside the fiber. How does this relate to quilting? If your chosen fabric crocks, the fabric will continually lose color in use and washing. Over time, the fabric will appear frosted or streaked, much like old worn denim jeans.

❋ *Washfastness* is the ability of a fabric to stand up to water and to the chemicals in detergents. Water temperature, the presence of chlorine, contact with another fabric, and reactions to chemicals in detergents all need to be considered. If the quilt will never be washed, you do not have to consider any of these issues. However, most quilts are used and require laundering once in a while, which means you need to know how the fabric will respond.

TO PREWASH OR NOT TO PREWASH

After reading the above definitions of the general problems fabrics have with color retention, you will need to decide whether to prewash or not. If you think that prewashing fabric will eliminate all of the above possibilities, you are thinking in the wrong direction. Instead, the decision of how to treat the fabric should be based on each fabric's characteristics and on the dyestuff used to color it.

tip One good reason not to prewash is that the finish on the fabric as it comes off the bolt can slow down the fading of the folds while the fabric is in storage.

Three important factors should be considered when washing cotton fabric or a finished quilt:

❋ *Water temperature:* Did you know that water temperature affects cotton fabric's ability to retain its color? Cotton fabrics perform best when the water temperature is between 80°F and 85°F ("cold" water). Any warmer, and, with the problematic colors mentioned earlier, a faint amount of color can start to appear in the water.

❋ *Chlorine:* Did you know that the normal amounts of chlorine found in processed tap water can cause some dyes to release their color? If you can smell chlorine in your tap water, there is enough present to cause many batiks, as well as jewel tones and dark colors, to bleed.

❋ *Detergent:* Did you know that the chlorine content of some detergents can damage the binders that hold the pigments to the surface of the cloth and can be harmful to some fiber-reactive dyes? Ivory and Dreft detergents, Ivory Dishwashing Liquid, and Orvus Paste are four excellent, safe choices for washing cotton fabrics.

Safe detergents for cotton fabric

FRONT-LOADING WASHERS

Be sure to consult your owner's manual if you own a front-loading washer, as these detergents are very concentrated and high-sudsing. Front-loading washers need low-suds detergents. If you have a front loader, talk to the manufacturer about the appropriate detergents to use. You will also need to test any recommended products with the fabrics you are using. Carrie and I both own top-loading machines, so we are not qualified to address the problems you might be up against with detergents and accessibility to the process once the door locks.

To test the washfastness of a fabric, perform this quick test: Fill a 2-cup glass measuring cup with 80°–85°F water. Dissolve 1 teaspoon of Ivory or Orvus detergent in the water. Pin a 3″ square of the fabric about which you're concerned to a 3″ piece of bleached muslin or a 3″ square of the lightest fabric from your quilt, and submerge them in the solution. Stir for 6–8 minutes. If you see no color in the water or if there is color in the water but not on the white fabric, you are probably safe with this water temperature and detergent. If you see color in the water and the white fabric has taken in the color, the fabric is bleeding and needs to be treated (or you need to choose another fabric).

Testing for bleeding

Color transferring onto white fabric

What do you do if you have a fabric that you feel you must use, but it has a colorfast problem? One, or a combination, of three chemicals can be used—Synthrapol, Retayne, or Carbona Color Run Remover. All are available in quilt shops and fabric stores.

Synthrapol is a chemical that removes unbonded dye molecules from fabrics. It is normally used to wash the excess dye out of fabric that has just been dyed. You can also use it to try to remove dye stains once they do occur. For example, if you wash your quilt for the first time and see dye stains on fabrics where they don't belong, *do not* dry the quilt. Immediately rewash it, following the instructions on the Synthrapol bottle; chances are the stains will be removed.

Color Run Remover is made specifically to remove colors that run during washing mishaps, like the classic red sock thrown in with the whites.

Retayne is used to "lock" colors that have been improperly processed, so they will stop bleeding and retain their color. It is used to set dye that continues to run and bleed in pre-testing. It is especially effective on reds, maroons, and batiks.

note *If you use any of these chemical products, you are preshrinking your fabric, because you are placing it in hot water to set the color. We strongly recommend that you do not mix prewashed and nonwashed fabrics together in the same quilt. Therefore, if you prewash one fabric in a project, you will need to prewash all the fabrics.*

Products for colorfast problems

Finally, in the laundry section of many grocery stores you will find Shout Color Catcher sheets and Carbona Dye Grabber cloths. These products are coated with a surface-action agent that absorbs loose dye and grime so they are not redeposited on fabrics or clothes in the wash. However, these products are only an extra precaution against potential problems with water or detergents; they do not eliminate the need to understand the properties of each fabric with which you work.

For much more thorough information on the colorfastness of fabrics and testing procedures, Harriet's book *From Fiber to Fabric* is now available as an e-book from C&T Publishing (see Resources, page 112).

LESSON THREE:
Fabric Preparation

If you have not read Volume 1, you should refer to it now, paying special attention to Class 120, Lessons One through Three (pages 12–17), where we taught you how to tear fabric to establish the crosswise grain and how to straighten the grain before cutting.

In this lesson, we address a couple of problems that you may be having after straightening the grain for cutting your strips. We also cover options for folding and determining strip length.

DO YOU HAVE V's IN YOUR STRIPS?

Carrie's way of working with strips is to measure over a distance of three or four strips. For example, if you want to end up with 1½" strips, measure 6" from the fabric's cut edge. Make the cut. Then move the ruler back 1½" and make another cut, move back another 1½" and cut, and so on. You will end up with four strips that should be straight. Repeat this process down the length of the fabric until you have your desired number of strips, or down the length of a strip set until you have the number of segments needed.

Another method of cutting strips

WORKING WITH FAT QUARTERS

Fat quarters are like candy for quilters. They are fun, compact, and easy to buy. A fat quarter is a half-yard of fabric cut in half on the fold. Each fat quarter measures 18" × 22". These little pieces are great to buy if you fall in love with a fabric and just need to possess it but have no real intention of using it for a quilt project (unless you are really into scrap quilting). We would, however, like to caution you about getting caught up in buying fat quarters for your projects. If you do the math as to what a fat quarter costs you, it is anywhere between $10 and $12 per yard, where the same fabric cut off the bolt would only cost between $9 and $10 per yard. As you learned in Volume 1 (page 13), fabric that is cut from the bolt instead of torn will probably not be on the straight of grain. Because the majority of quilt shops cut their fabric, your fat quarters are also going to be cut. So, by the time you tear off your strips to get the fabric on the straight of grain, your fat quarter may be considerably reduced in size.

All that being said, if you have a bunch of fat quarters and need small yardages for a project, a fat quarter may be just the ticket. Just as you learned in Volume 1 (page 16), you will need to straighten your fabric so that it is on-grain. Unlike working with 45" material, however, with fat quarters you only have 22". If you have cut fat quarters, you still need to tear off a strip that is at least ½" wider than the size strip needed so you can determine the fabric's grainline. Start your tear by making a clip in the cut edge opposite the selvage. Depending on how far off-grain your fabric is, you may be able to tear off a small amount of fabric on the other side of the fat quarter, or you may need to tear off another piece that is at least as wide as the strips you will be cutting.

> *note* Because most patterns for quilts work with yardage cut from a 45"-wide bolt of fabric (unless using fat quarters is specified), you will need to double the number of strips needed, as you have only half the width.

Straightening an off-grain fat quarter

Now you will iron and straighten your fat quarter just like you would a full 45″-wide piece of fabric. However, you will only need to fold the fabric once—the cut edge, opposite the selvage, up to the selvage, making sure that your torn edges are completely aligned.

Fat quarter folded and ready to cut

SHORT STRIPS FROM HALF- AND QUARTER-YARD CUTS

As you make more and more quilts, you may begin to be enticed by scrap quilts. The problem with scrap quilts, however, is the large number of fabrics needed for variety.

Instead of cutting long 42″ strips crosswise, then cutting them into pieces for your scrap quilt, why not cut them shorter in the first place? If you work with half-yard pieces (18″) or quarter-yard pieces (9″), the strips will be cut lengthwise, making them more stable than crosswise cuts. This idea was originally introduced in 1992 by Judy Martin, who named the 18″ strips Short Strips and the 9″ strips Mini Strips.

When making scrap quilts, you may not want to use a 45″ strip of any one fabric. Instead, try layering four different fat quarters or half-yards, aligning the selvages (lengthwise grain). You can then cut four different 18″ strips in one stroke. If you want the maximum scrap variety, use quarter-yards for Mini Strips, which are just 9″ long. Layering four fabrics offers the further advantage of easier alignment and more precise cutting because *there is no fold*. This fact alone can make a big difference in your accuracy.

Fat quarters stacked up to cut four at a time

Short Strips cut on the lengthwise grain can be made using the same strip dimensions used for crosswise strips. Simply make the first cut parallel to the selvage. If you are following a pattern that calls for 42″ strips, the yardage should be approximately the same for Short Strips. You will need 2½ times as many 18″ strips to yield the same number of patches cut from 42″-long strips.

LESSON FOUR:
Review of basic principles

Following is a list of the basic piecing principles that we covered in detail in Volume 1.

1. Always work on the straight of grain, either lengthwise or crosswise. Be sure that you have torn both ends of your yardage and have realigned the crosswise grain of all the pieces before you begin to cut. (Volume 1, Class 120, Lesson Three, page 15)

2. Accurate cutting is the beginning of your success or frustration as you piece. Be sure to use the correct ruler for the job. You should also work with a single brand of ruler that you can easily read and stay accurate. (Volume 1, Class 120, Lessons Four and Five, pages 17–19)

3. Find your personal accurate seam allowances. Remember that ¼″ seam allowances don't work. Set up a system on your machine that allows you to have accurate finished units, not perfect seam allowances. (Volume 1, Class 130, Lessons One and Two, pages 20–23)

4. Pressing can make or break your quilt top. Therefore, it is one of the most important processes to master. Proper pressing leads to flat, straight, extremely accurate pieced tops. (Volume 1, Class 130, Lesson Four, page 26)

5. Trim for accuracy. After you sew and press each seam, align a ruler on the seam and check that the strip measurement from the seam to the raw edge is exact. This prevents all the small distortions that occur when cutting, sewing, and pressing. (Volume 1, Class 130, Lesson Five, page 28)

Class 230

We are now going to enter into the world of settings. Volume 1 addressed the basics of accurate piecing, using simple blocks and straight, horizontal settings. You had enough to learn in getting excellent results piecing the blocks without worrying about settings.

No amount of artistic analysis will help you understand why certain quilts are more appealing to you than others. However, as you explore the settings in this book, you may discover that the fancy blocks aren't always the ones that catch your eye; rather, your eye is often drawn to the manner in which the blocks are set together. The quilts that tend to be the most satisfying to look at are the ones that have blocks set to their best advantage. The next time you go to a quilt show, or look in a book, study the ones that you return to again and again. Although art quilts get much more attention than do traditional quilts, a great number of traditional quilts express the best of the quiltmaking tradition—repeated blocks and patterns that have motion and coherence, beauty, sparkle, and warmth. These attributes are in the quilts that you would like to live with for years, the quilt that you would like to have on your bed or on

a wall, the ones that are passed on to the next generation.

Our plan is for you to start exploring all the different possibilities early in your quiltmaking experience. Different arrangements of quilt blocks will change their look dramatically. So, take the time and explore all your possibilities as you work through this book.

LESSON ONE:
What is a diagonal set?

Diagonal sets are often referred to as "on-point" settings. If your blocks seem plain and unexciting, try setting them on-point for a whole new perspective: "If in doubt, set it on-point." Setting blocks on-point significantly changes the graphics, and the overall effect can be quite different. Horizontal lines are restful; diagonal lines are dramatic and visually more exciting than horizontal ones.

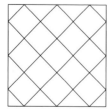

Basic diagonal set

When designing your diagonal set, try different options. Often a very interesting secondary pattern emerges when the same block is set next to another of itself. Look closely at this next illustration. The same block is used throughout; the only difference is the change of color position. This is actually a positive/negative color set-up within the block. Can you see the block?

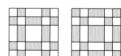

The same block (positive/negative) set side by side

Wonderful secondary patterns also emerge when two different blocks are alternated in the setting.

Alternating blocks set side by side

There are two different ways to set blocks side by side. The illustration below shows one block in the corner and continues with successive odd-numbered rows. Once the quilt top arrives at the planned width, the rows can continue at that number of blocks until the desired length is achieved; they are then decreased successively.

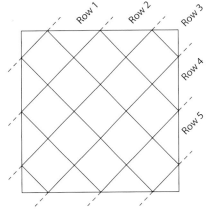

Single block in the corner setting.
Row 3 can repeat for a rectangular quilt.

Another type of diagonal set begins with two blocks in the first row, continues adding two blocks to each row, and continues with even-numbered rows until the top is lengthened beyond a square. The rows then decrease by two even numbers.

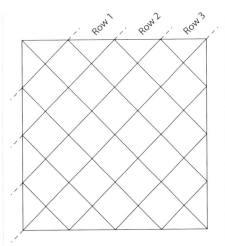

Two blocks in corner setting

A plain alternate block can also be added, enhancing the space surrounding the blocks. These plain blocks also offer a wonderful place for elaborate quilting designs to be stitched.

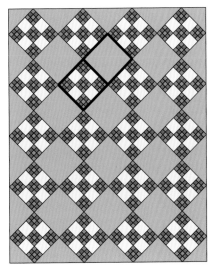

Diagonal set with plain alternate block

Class 250 includes worksheets (pages 55–63) to help you figure out different design ideas. The blocks in the worksheets are 1″ square, which means it's easy to work on ⅛″- or ¼″-grid graph paper. This is a fun way to mock up quilt ideas.

Diagonal sets are no more difficult to construct than straight sets. However, there are some technical differences. When the blocks are set into a

diagonal orientation, you end up with triangle spaces around the edges. For your quilt to have straight sides, you must cut large triangles, called side-setting triangles, and corner triangles to fit into those spaces. You need either a formula or a special ruler to make the triangles the correct size and have the straight of grain along the outside edges.

Don't overlook the idea of making the side-setting triangles and corners from a fabric that contrasts with the rest of the quilt, creating a "frame" around your pieced blocks. *Nine-Patch on Point* (page 29), *Irish Garden* (page 34), and *Five-Patch Chain* (page 67) all utilize this design element.

LESSON TWO:

Figuring for setting triangles

Many quilters feel that diagonal set quilts are difficult because of the math required to determine the size of the side-setting triangles. Many antique quilts and early quilt books show that the triangles were made from a square of fabric the size of the blocks with seam allowances added for the diagonal cut. This square was then cut in half and sewn onto the row to make the edge. The problem with this method is that the entire edge of the quilt is bias and that the quilt will never lie flat and straight. For a quilt to lie flat, you want the edges and corners to be on the straight of grain.

Two different triangles are needed to fill in the edges of your quilt. The corner triangles are marked C on the illustration, and the side triangles are marked S. Corner triangles are exactly one-fourth the size of a finished block, while side triangles are exactly one-half of a finished block. (The shaded areas on the illustration represent the size relationship between the triangles and the blocks).

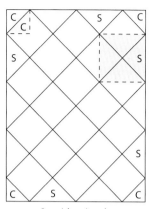

S = side triangle
C = corner triangle

We are giving you three different methods for determining the size to cut the side-setting triangles. These methods ensure that the outside edges of the quilt top will be on the straight of grain, giving the top the most stability.

❈ METHOD A
(MATHEMATICALLY CORRECT)

SIDE TRIANGLES

The short sides of the side triangles should have the same measurement as the blocks in the quilt top. To cut this triangle without a special ruler or template and still obtain straight of grain on the outside edge of the quilt top, you need to determine the measurement of its long side. To do so, multiply the short side times 1.414. Then, add 1¼″ for seam allowances to that measurement. Cut a square this size and then cut twice, from corner to corner diagonally.

Short side × 1.414 = long side

Long side + 1¼″ = size to cut square

Let's try this out. Assume you have 6″-square finished blocks (remember, we always use the finished size when doing the calculations).

6″ × 1.414 = 8.48″ + 1.25″ = 9.73″, or in ruler language, 9¾″

You would cut a 9¾″ square, and then cut that square from corner to corner twice.

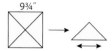

Side setting triangles for 6″ blocks with straight grain on outer edge of quilt

CORNER TRIANGLES

The length of the long side of the corner triangle is the same as the block size in the quilt. To cut this triangle without a special ruler or template and still obtain straight of grain in the right position, we need to determine the measurements of the short sides.

To do so, divide the long side by 1.414. Then, add ⅞″ (.875) to that measurement for seam allowances. Cut a square this size and then cut once, corner to corner.

Long side ÷ 1.414 = short side

Short side + ⅞″ = size to cut square

Again, using a 6″ finished block:

6″ ÷ 1.414 = 4.243″ + .875″ = 5.118″, which in ruler-friendly numbers is 5⅛″

So, to get all four corner triangles with the straight of grain in the right position, you would cut two squares 5⅛″ square. Then cut each square diagonally, from corner to corner.

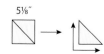

Corner setting triangles for 6″ blocks

tip To sum up Method A: To find the measurements for side triangles, multiply the finished size of the block by 1.414 and add 1¼″. Cut a square this size, and cut it twice, corner to corner. To find the measurement for the corner triangles, divide the finished block size by 1.414 and add ⅞″. Cut a square this size, and cut it once, corner to corner.

note *Refer to the Decimal Equivalents chart when converting to fractions. For setting triangles, it's usually recommended that you round up, rather than down, to get to a nice number.*

Decimal Equivalents

Decimal	Fraction	Decimal	Fraction
.0625	¹⁄₁₆	.5625	⁹⁄₁₆
.1	¹⁄₁₀	.5714	⁴⁄₇
.125	⅛	.6	⅗
.1428	¹⁄₇	.625	⅝
.1666	⅙	.6666	⅔
.1875	³⁄₁₆	.6875	¹¹⁄₁₆
.2	⅕	.7	⁷⁄₁₀
.25	¼	.7142	⁵⁄₇
.2857	²⁄₇	.75	¾
.3	³⁄₁₀	.8	⅘
.3125	⁵⁄₁₆	.8125	¹³⁄₁₆
.3333	⅓	.833	⅚
.375	⅜	.8571	⁶⁄₇
.4	⅖	.875	⅞
.4285	³⁄₇	.9	⁹⁄₁₀
.4375	⁷⁄₁₆	.9375	¹⁵⁄₁₆
.5	½		

❋ METHOD B (SPACE TO PLAY)

Method A gives you triangles that are exactly the size needed to achieve a straight edge, extending only ¼″ (seam allowance) away from the points of the blocks. There are times, however, when you may want the background fabric to extend beyond the points of the blocks, perhaps to float the blocks or give additional space for quilting. In that case, you would do the math a bit differently. This method, credited to Mary Ellen Hopkins, was first introduced in her book *It's Okay if You Sit on My Quilt.*

To find the size of the square that will be cut into quarters for the side triangles, add a minimum of 3″ to the diagonal measurement of the finished design block.

We will use a 6″ block as an example. From the Diagonal Measurements for Blocks chart, you can see that the diagonal of a 6″ square is 8.48″ (6 × 1.414 = 8.48), or a ruler-happy number of 8½″. Add 3″ to 8½″ to get 11½″. Cut the squares needed for the sides to 11½″, then cut them into quarters from corner to corner.

Diagonal Measurements for Blocks

Square	Diagonal	Square	Diagonal
1.5″	2.12″	11	15.55
2	2.83	12	16.97
3	4.24	13	18.38
4	5.66	14	19.8
5	7.07	15	21.21
6	8.48	16	22.62
7	9.9	17	24.04
8	11.31	18	25.45
9	12.73	19	26.87
10	14.14	20	28.28

NOTE: These measurements can be rounded off in either direction.

For the corners, cut two squares at least 2″ larger than the side measurement of the finished block. Thus, for a 6″ block, you would cut two 8″ squares. Cut the squares in half diagonally. You now have four corners with the proper grain placement.

Use the two handy reference charts to determine the sizes. One shows exact sizes and the other shows floating sizes for some standard-sized blocks.

Sizes for Exact Corner and Side Triangles

Original Block Measurement	Size to Cut Side Setting Triangle	Size to Cut Corner Setting Triangle
6″	9¾″	5⅛″
7″	11⅛″	5⅞″
8″	12½″	6½″
9″	14″	7¼″
10″	15⅜″	8″
11″	16¾″	8¾″
12″	18¼″	9⅜″

Sizes for Floating Corner and Side Triangles

Original Block Measurement	Diagonal Measurement (rounded up)	Size to Cut for Side Triangles	Size to Cut for Corner Triangles
6″	8½″	11½″	8″
7″	10″	13″	9″
8″	11½″	14½″	10″
9″	12¾″	15¾″	11″
10″	14¼″	17¼″	12″
11″	15½″	18½″	13″
12″	17″	20″	14″

> *note* When you sew the triangles onto the rows, you may find that the act of sewing creates stress on the bias edges, causing the outside edges to curve inward. If you cut the triangles exactly the right size, as in Method A, they might curve in enough after sewing that you no longer have a straight edge. There is no way to straighten that edge, because there is no extra fabric to work with. If you make the triangles oversized as in Method B, you can trim them down to any distance from the corner seams you prefer.

❋ METHOD C (USING SPECIAL RULERS)

Now that you have worked through the math techniques, you might find that this is a bit too much for you. If so, try out some of the specialty rulers made specifically for figuring out these triangles. The Setting Triangles ruler, invented by Lynn Graves, does most of the work for you. It determines the size strip you need to cut based on the size of your unfinished block. You can then cut your triangles from a strip instead of a square. Everything you need for doing this is marked on the ruler.

Creative Grids also offers nonslip side-setting triangle rulers. These rulers are available in mini size (blocks that finish 1"–6") and the standard size (for blocks that finish 6"–12"). Like the Setting Triangle ruler, they allow you to cut strips of fabric instead of squares. Use the rectangular end of the ruler to cut strips the right width for the side-setting triangles that will match the size of your blocks. Then use the triangular end of the ruler to cut the triangles. The math is built into the ruler, so you only need to know the size of your block.

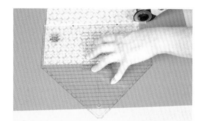

Using the Creative Grids Setting Triangle Ruler to cut strips

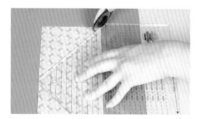

Using the Creative Grids Setting Triangle Ruler to cut triangles

LESSON THREE:
Basic layout and sewing

The sewing used to piece blocks into a diagonal set is a bit different from that used to piece a straight set. The blocks are sewn together into diagonal rows. The addition of side triangles requires you to plan their placement and orientation in the row before you sew them to the row.

It is extremely helpful to position the blocks on a design wall before sewing everything together. Once it is all on the wall, stand back and check that all the blocks are in the proper position. Otherwise, you will find that it is easy to get things turned around a bit when sewing the rows.

When everything is the way you like it, sew together the blocks in each diagonal row, adding the side-setting triangles to the ends of each row, aligning the right-angle corner of the triangle with the corner of the block. Once all the blocks are joined, trim the corners of the side-setting triangles before sewing the rows together.

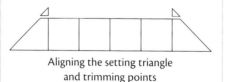

Aligning the setting triangle and trimming points

We recommend that you sew all the rows together before you add the four corner triangles. If you used Method A to make your triangles, it won't matter whether you sew the corner triangles during row construction or at the end, because they are cut to the exact size. If you used Method B, you need to attach the corner triangles last, to give the seams unity and balance. If you always add the corner triangles last, you don't have to be concerned when it matters and when it doesn't.

Sewing diagonally set blocks into rows

Looking at the illustration, you will see that the right-angle points of the triangles are kept on the same line as the block edges, whereas the sharper points of the triangles overhang the block. It is important to keep this edge straight. In Volume 1, you learned to stack all the blocks into rows, take them to your machine, and chain sew them all at once (page 29). This method can become a bit tricky for diagonal sets. In the illustration, you can see that the rows have a different number of blocks and the angle of the side-setting triangles changes from the top half to the bottom. Therefore, we suggest that the first few times you construct a diagonal set quilt, you work with one row at a time, pressing and trimming the points and placing that row back in position before picking up the next row. Once you are comfortable with the process, you can pin the triangles in the correct position to their adjoining blocks and pick up more than one row at a time.

Once you have sewn all the blocks and setting triangles into rows, sew the rows together. We suggest constructing the two halves of the quilt top and then joining the halves. After the halves are joined, add the corner triangles.

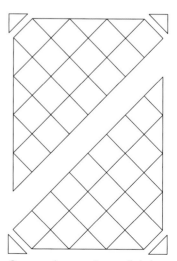

Constructing rows into quilt halves

IMPORTANT THINGS TO REMEMBER

Before you start sewing again, let's review some very important processes that were covered in Volume 1 to make sure that your piecing is the best it can be. Accurate cutting and sewing are the basis of your success.

When you start a new project, don't forget to *test your seam allowance*. Using the fabrics of the new project, cut three strips of fabric 1½" × 6". Sew two strips together and press. Check the width of each strip and trim if necessary. Attach the third strip and press. Measure the center strip; it should measure 1" exactly. If it doesn't, adjust your seam allowance as needed. (Volume 1, Class 130, Lesson Three, page 25)

Be sure that the raw **edges of each piece are even and matched.** You should not see either fabric peeking beyond the cut edge you are sewing. (Volume 1, Class 130, Lesson Five, page 27)

Slow down. So often we think that because we are working on a machine, we should sew fast. But you should go slow enough that the sewing machine needle enters and exits the fabric exactly where you want it to.

Keep the sewing straight. Most sewing machines tend to pull the fabric to the left as you approach the end of the seam, making the seam allowance narrower and causing a flare to the unit when pressing. Make sure that you enter the fabric at your exact seam allowance and exit at the exact same distance. To do this, sit directly in front of the needle of the machine so that your vision is straight onto the needle and your seam guide system. A stiletto or similar tool, as well as a straight stitch throat plate, can help you hold the edges in place as you get to the end of a seam.

Measure and trim as you go. This one action gives you the highest probability of accuracy. Never sew several strips together at once. Instead, sew two strips or units together, press, and measure to check for exact accuracy. Trim if necessary, or resew if the units are coming up too small. With the addition of each new strip or unit, repeat the process. (Volume 1, Class 130, Lesson Five, page 28)

Press, press, press!! We can't stress this enough. Using starch and pressing accurately both help keep your work flat and clean as you progress. (Volume 1, Class 130, Lesson Four, page 26)

hint *When bias edges are stitched to straight edges, sew with the bias edge on the feed dogs (bottom) to prevent it from stretching.*

Until the constructed quilt top is basted and quilted, it is fragile and can easily be stretched out of square. The bias grain of the fabric runs the length and width of the quilt top, making it a bit like a rubber band. Starch can really be an added help when constructing diagonal sets, as the stiffness counteracts the extreme stretch that naturally occurs with this setting. Take extra care when folding or hanging your quilt top. The center can be stretched out of square, making it difficult to get it to lie flat again. We suggest that for stability, you layer and baste diagonal set quilt tops as soon as they are finished.

LESSON FOUR:
Finishing the sampler

The sampler quilt

It is now time to finish the sampler that we started in Volume 1. The sides containing the Nine-Patch blocks are your exercise for trying your hand at diagonal sets. There are four borders needed. The Nine-Patch blocks appear to be floating in the white fabric. This design was necessary to make the border unit as wide as the corner squares.

Use Method B (page 25) to determine the sizes needed for the setting triangles and corners. The Nine-Patch blocks were created on a 1″ grid, which means each is a 3″ block:

3″ × 1.414 = 4.24″, rounded up equals 4.25″. 4.25″ + 3″ = 7.25″

So, you need to cut four 7¼″ squares from the background fabric for side-setting triangles. Then, cut the four squares in half diagonally twice, corner to corner.

For the corner squares, the side measurement is 3″. (3″ + 2″ = 5″.) Cut eight 5″ squares and cut them in half diagonally once.

Follow the diagram to help you lay out one side border. You will use four side-setting triangles and four corner triangles for each border unit.

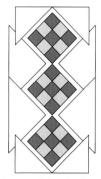

Nine-Patch border layout

Sew the side setting triangles onto the Nine-Patch blocks. Notice that the center Nine-Patch block has a setting triangle on both sides, while the top and bottom blocks have only one side-setting triangle on one side. Press the seams toward the triangles. Trim the points. Repeat for the remaining three borders.

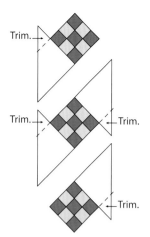

Position of side-setting triangles

Next, join these Nine-Patch units together.

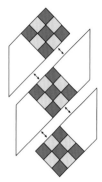

Join Nine-Patch units

To add the first two corner triangles, fold each triangle in half to find the center point and center with the middle square of one Nine-Patch, on each end. Press toward the triangle.

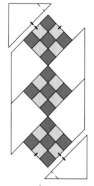

Placement of corner triangles

Trim off the points of the two triangles that extend beyond the Nine-Patch block where you will sew your next corner triangle.

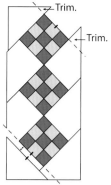

Trimming to sew on the last two corner triangles

Trim the borders to fit the Four-Patch corner units. The Four-Patch units measure 6½″ square unfinished, so the Nine-Patch borders will need to be trimmed to 6½″. The easiest way to do this is to place the 3¼″ measure line of your ruler on the points of the Nine-Patch blocks. Trim away the excess side-setting triangle fabric. Repeat for the opposite side and then repeat for the remaining three borders.

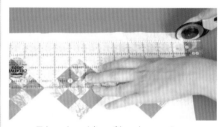

Trimming sides of border sections

Trim the length of the border to 14″. Use the same technique as above: Place the 7″ measure line through the center of the center Nine-Patch block and trim each end. Repeat for the remaining three borders.

Construct the quilt top like a big nine-patch: Sew the Four-Patch corner units onto the ends of two of the Nine-Patch border units. Press the seams toward the border. Then sew the remaining two border units onto the large Fence Post center section. Press the seams toward the borders. Now you are ready to sew the units together into a quilt top.

The quilts

PROJECT ONE: *NINE-PATCH ON POINT*

Quilt top size: 52″ × 52″

Grid size: 2″

Block size: 6″

Blocks:

16 blue and white

9 dark print and white

36 light print alternate squares

20 side-setting triangles

4 corner triangles

Yardages for quilt top:

⅔ yard white

1 yard dark print

⅜ yard blue

1⅛ yards light print

Nine-Patch on Point

> *note* Yardages given represent the actual yardage needed based on 42″ width. No allowances are added. Please add the amount that you are comfortable with for straightening and cutting.

Constructing the outer blocks

Cutting:

Nine-Patch block   Rows 1 and 3

Formula: 2 segments per block × 2½″ long = 5″ × 16 blocks = 80″ ÷ 42″ (width of fabric) = 1.90, rounded up to 2 strip sets

Cut:

4 strips 2½″ wide of the blue fabric

2 strips 2½″ wide of the white fabric

Row 2

Formula: 1 segment per block × 2½″ long = 2.5″ × 16 blocks = 40″, or 1 strip set

Cut:

2 strips 2½″ wide of the white fabric

1 strip 2½″ wide of the blue fabric

Construct the Nine-Patch blocks. Remember the steps? (Refer to Volume 1, Class 160, Lesson Three, page 74, if needed.)

1. Sew together the first 2 strips for each strip set.

2. Set the seam with steam; then press seam allowance over and starch.

3. Trim each strip so it is exactly 2¼″ wide.

4. Add the third strip. Press and starch. Then trim to 2¼″ wide.

5. The center strip should measure exactly 2″ wide.

6. Cut the strip sets into 2½″ segments, measuring from both internal seams for alignment.

7. Lay out all the blocks into stacks that are 16 deep. Stitch together the first 2 segments for all 16 blocks.

8. Fan the seams and press.

9. Check each side of the sewn unit for 2¼″ accuracy. Trim if necessary.

10. Add the third segment. Fan the seams and press.

11. Check that the block is exactly 6½″ square.

Body of the quilt

Cutting:

Nine-Patch block   Rows 1 and 3

Formula: 2 segments per block × 2½″ long = 5″ × 9 blocks = 45″, or 1 strip set plus a few inches of a second.

Cut:

2 strips 2½″ wide of the dark print

1 strip 2½″ wide of the white fabric

(Use leftover strips for the bit extra needed.)

Row 2

Formula: 1 segment per block × 2½″ long = 2.5″ × 9 blocks = 22.5″, or 1 strip set.

Cut:

2 strips 2½″ wide of the white fabric

1 strip 2½″ wide of the dark print

Construct 9 Nine-Patch blocks.

Alternate block

Formula:

36 squares 6½″ × 6½″ needed.

42″ ÷ 6.5 = 6 squares per strip.

36 ÷ 6 = 6 strips needed.

Cut:

6 strips 6½″ wide of the light print, then cut each into 6 –6½″ squares.

Lay out the blocks on a design wall or floor, using the illustration as a guide.

Block layout

> *tip*   Be sure to read page 26 if you are unfamiliar with this process.

Side-setting triangles

Use Method B (page 25) to determine the size needed for the side-setting triangles.

The blocks are 6″ square finished:

6″ × 1.414 = 8.48″, rounded up to 8.5″. 8.5″ + 3″ = 11.5″

The size of squares you need is 11½″. You need 20 triangles (five per side, each square yields four triangles):

20 triangles ÷ 4 = 5 squares.

42″ (width of fabric) ÷ 11.5 = 3 squares from each strip

Cut 2 strips 11½″ wide. Cut 5 squares 11½″, then cut them on the diagonal into quarters.

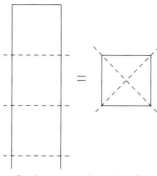

Cutting squares into triangles

1. On the design wall, position the setting triangles at the ends of each row.

2. Starting in the top left corner, stitch the triangles to the opposite sides of the solid square. Press toward the square.

3. For Row 2, stitch the 3 blocks together, pressing each seam allowance toward the solid square. Add the triangles to each end, making sure that they are turned correctly. Align the edges carefully. Stitch and press toward the square.

4. Repeat Step 3 until all 11 rows are constructed. Trim the points off the triangles to get a straight edge.

Row layout adding side triangles

5. Sew Row 1 and Row 2 together, butting the seams perfectly and keeping the setting triangles aligned with the blocks. Press the seam allowance. Continue until half of the quilt top is constructed (Rows 1–6).

6. Starting again at the opposite corner, repeat the process for the remaining 5 rows. Be sure to press and starch each seam as they are joined to keep the top straight and accurate.

7. Join the 2 halves together.

Corner triangles

1. Use Method B (page 25) to determine the size of the 4 corner triangles. The blocks measure 6″ finished – 6″ + 2″ = 8″. Cut 2 – 8″ squares. Cut each square in half diagonally once to get the four triangles needed for the corners.

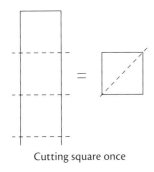

Cutting square once

2. Fold the long side of each triangle in half to find the center. Align the centers of the triangles with the centers of the blocks in the corners of the quilt top. Sew the four corners in place. Press toward the corners.

3. Refer to Class 280, Lesson One (page 96), for instructions on squaring the corners and straightening the edges.

PROJECT TWO: *METRO MAIN STREET*

Metro Main Street

Quilt top size: 50½″ × 50½″

Grid size: 1¼″

Block size: 3¾″

Blocks:

49 Nine-Patch blocks

4 Fence Post blocks each in dark, medium, and light teal print

16 Fence Post blocks in dark and medium teal print combination

8 Fence Post blocks in medium and light teal print combination

24 side-setting triangles

4 corner triangles

Yardages for quilt top:

½ yard white print for Nine-Patch blocks

½ yard brown print for Nine-Patch blocks

¼ yard chocolate brown for center of Nine-Patch blocks

¾ yard light paisley for setting triangles and middle of Fence Post blocks

⅛ yard light teal for Fence Post blocks

¼ yard medium teal for Fence Post blocks

¼ yard dark teal for Fence Post blocks

note Yardages given represent the actual yardage needed based on 42″ width. No allowances are added. Please add the amount that you are comfortable with for straightening and cutting.

In this fun quilt, you use only Nine-Patch blocks and Fence Post blocks to create a flowing circular secondary pattern. Play with your color placement by drawing out the quilt as you learned in Volume 1, Class 150 (page 54).

Body of the quilt

Cutting:

Let's start with the Nine-Patch blocks. You need two different strip sets to create these blocks.

Nine-Patch block   Strip Set A: Rows 1 and 3

Formula: 49 blocks × 2 segments per block = 98 segments needed × 1¾″ for each segment = 171.5″ ÷ 42″ = 4.08 strip sets needed. For the white print, round this up to 4½ because you need twice as much of it as the brown print.

Cut:

9 strips 1¾″ wide of the white print

5 strips 1¾″ wide of the brown print

(Set aside the extra half strip of brown print, as you will use it for strip set B.)

Strip Set B: Row 2

Formula: 49 blocks × 1 segment per block = 49 segments needed × 1¾″ for each segment = 85.75″ ÷ 42″ = 2.04 strip sets. For safety this should be rounded up to 2½ strip sets.

Cut:

5 strips 1¾″ wide of the brown print (plus the extra half strip you set aside previously)

3 strips 1¾″ wide of the chocolate brown

Because this is the only place that chocolate brown is used in the quilt, you may want to cut only two strips and see if you can squeeze that extra 0.04 from the end of one of the strip sets; if you can't, then you can cut another strip.

Construct 9 Nine-Patch blocks using the guidelines laid out in the *Nine-Patch on Point* project (page 29).

Next, you need to make the alternate blocks.

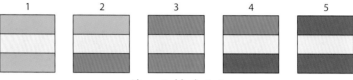

Alternate blocks 1–5

The alternate block for this quilt is a pieced Fence Post block. For a bit of a challenge, we used five different color combinations to create the quilt's secondary pattern. The center of all the Fence Post blocks is the same—a light paisley fabric. The quilt center consists of four blocks in which the outer two strips are a light teal (block 1). The next ring out from the center consists of eight blocks that have one outer strip in light teal and the other in medium teal (block 2), as well as four blocks with medium teal for both the outer strips (block 3). The final round consists of sixteen Fence Post blocks with one outer strip being the medium teal again and the other a dark teal print (block 4), as well as four blocks in the corners that are made of just the paisley and the dark teal print (block 5).

Formula for alternate blocks 1, 3, and 5: 4 blocks of each strip set; 4 × 4¼″ long = 17″ ÷ 42″ = 0.4 strips or half a strip set for each of these color combinations.

Cut:

2 strips of the light paisley

1 strip each of the light, medium, and dark teal (then cut in half)

Formula for alternate block 2: 8 blocks of the strip set: 8 blocks × 4¼″ cut size = 34″ ÷ 42″ = 0.8, or only 1 strip set.

Cut:

1 strip of the light teal

1 strip of the light paisley

1 strip of the medium teal

Formula for alternate block 4: 16 blocks of the strip set: 16 blocks × 4¼″ cut size = 68″ ÷ 42″ = 1.62 strips, or 2 strip sets

Cut:

2 strips of the medium teal

2 strips of the light paisley

2 strips of the dark teal

Construct the Fence Post blocks. Remember the steps? (Refer to Volume 1, Class 130, Lessons Five and Six, pages 27–32, if needed.)

1. Sew the first two strips together for each strip set.

2. Press the seam allowance; starch and press dry on the right side of the strip.

3. Trim each strip so it is exactly 1½″ wide.

4. Add the third strip. Press and starch. The trim to 1½″ wide.

5. The center strip should measure exactly 1¼″ wide.

6. Cut the strip sets into 4¼″ segments, measuring from both internal seams for alignment.

7. Once all the blocks are constructed, lay out the blocks on the design wall or floor, using the illustration as a guide.

Block layout

Side setting triangles

Use Method B (page 25) to determine the size needed for the side-setting triangles.

The blocks are 3¾″ square finished:

3¾″ × 1.414 = 5.3″, rounded up to 5.5″

5.5″ + 2.5″ = 8″ squares

There are 24 triangles (six per side). Each square yields four triangles.

24 triangles ÷ 4 = 6 squares

42″ ÷ 8″ = 5.25, or 5 squares from each strip

Cut 2 strips 8″ wide. Cut 6 squares 8″, and then cut them on the diagonal into quarters.

1. On the design wall, position the setting triangles at the ends of each row. Once your blocks are laid out, you can start to pick up the rows and piece them together.

2. Starting in the top left corner, stitch the triangles to the opposite sides of the Nine-Patch in the corner. Press toward the triangle.

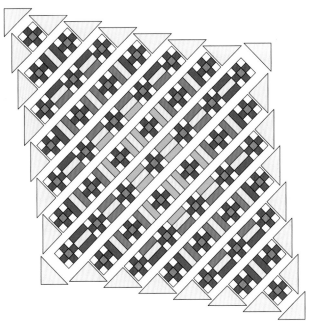

Row layout adding side triangles

3. For Row 2, stitch together the three blocks, pressing each seam allowance toward the Fence Post block. Add the triangles to each end, making sure that they are turned correctly. Align the edges carefully. Stitch and press toward the triangles.

4. Repeat Step 3 until all 13 rows are constructed. Trim the points off the triangles to get a straight edge.

5. Sew Row 1 and Row 2 together, butting the seams perfectly and keeping the setting triangles straight with the blocks. Press the seam allowance. Continue until one half of the top is constructed (Rows 1–7).

6. Starting again at the opposite corner, repeat the process for the remaining six rows. Be sure to press and starch each seam as they are joined to keep the top straight and accurate.

7. Join the two halves.

8. Use Method B (page 25) to determine the size of the four corner triangles. The blocks measure 3¾″ finished: 3¾″ + 2″ = 5¾″. Cut 2 – 5¾″ squares. Cut each square in half diagonally once to get the four triangles needed for the corners.

9. Fold the long side of each triangle in half to find the center. Align the centers of the triangles with the centers of the blocks in the corners of the quilt top. Sew the four corners in place. Press toward the corners.

10. Refer to Class 280, Lesson One (page 96), for instructions on squaring the corners and straightening the edges.

Alternate: *Irish Garden*

Irish Garden is a smaller version of *Metro Main Street* that you can make as an alternative. For this quilt, Carrie used a different color for the side and corner setting triangles. Have fun with the color of your setting triangles, as it can really set your quilt off nicely!

Irish Garden

Class 240

LESSON ONE:

Improving your workspace

If you are gradually finding more space to claim for your quilting, this lesson will help you set it up to accommodate your electrical and lighting needs.

ELECTRICAL NEEDS

When planning your workspace, don't overlook the electrical needs of your equipment. When sewing machines, irons, computers, task lights, televisions, and stereos are used simultaneously, they create a large power draw. Kitchens are wired for such power usage, but bedrooms, living rooms, family rooms, and basements generally are not. Therefore, you need to check the amps available to the room you're planning to use.

Kitchens usually combine four receptacles on one 20-amp circuit. This is sufficient to carry multiple appliances at once. Bedrooms, on the other hand, can combine lights and outlets on one less-powerful 15-amp circuit, often sharing this circuit with more than one room. Plug an iron into an outlet in one room, and it might borrow power from other rooms, causing lights to dim and motors to turn more

slowly than they should. You may want to consult with an electrician and consider increasing the size of the wire and the capacity of the circuits or putting the lights on a different circuit, if possible.

Start by determining the power requirements you need in your workspace. Think about the activities you will be performing at the same time in the room. We iron as we construct, leaving the iron on all day. We might also watch television or listen to the stereo while we work. A computer is also often part of the plan, and it's likely to be on while we work. How many lights will be on all at once, and will you need a space heater? A little math allows you to determine all your needs.

Find the wattage that each item requires and divide it by 120 (the average household outlet voltage). The answer to this inquiry is the number of amps needed to run the item or to light the bulb. The iron is a quilter's biggest user of power. To see just how much is needed to run it continuously, try this example: The average iron is rated at 1200 watts. Divide 1,200 by 120, and you see that it takes 10 amps to run the iron (and even more to heat it up). The average sewing machine requires 1–2 amps, as does a stereo,

television, VCR, computer, or light. Add a printer, which can need up to 6 amps, and the power needs really add up. The standard 15-amp circuit can run five to seven 1- to 2-amp items. Add an iron on the same circuit and an overload could occur, which could damage a computerized sewing machine.

Once you add up your needs, consider having two circuits for your sewing space: one 20-amp circuit for your iron and one 15-amp circuit for everything else. If you're putting in a new outlet for the iron, consider installing it where you'll be ironing and at a height that makes efficient use of the cord. If this is not possible, hire an electrician to examine your space and see if the electrical load can be rebalanced. If not, find out which outlets share a circuit breaker or fuse, then use an extension cord to plug the iron into a different circuit in a different location. Be sure that the extension cord has molded plug and socket ends, is no longer than 25 feet, and is made of 16-gauge wire.

If you have a computer in your sewing space, remember that it requires consistent power but not much of it. It is vital that you use a surge protector to protect your computer. When purchasing a strip surge protector, make sure that it is rated at a minimum of 15 amps. Another consideration is to use only one motor per circuit. Avoid plugging your sewing machine into a circuit that another motorized piece of equipment is using. If this is unavoidable, do not operate both at the same time. By analyzing your power needs, you can determine what changes need to be made in your room's circuits before they create trouble for you.

Electrical outlets should be readily available to eliminate the need for extension cords running across the floor. Strip outlets mounted on the wall are one possibility when you need additional plugs in one area. Coiled, expandable extension cords, mounted from the ceiling using a drapery rod, allow an electrical item, such as an iron, to be plugged in and moved from place to place without your having to worry about where the cord is. If you are starting from scratch, don't overlook placing outlets in the floor.

DYNADISC

If you do not have a good, supportive office chair, a simple, inexpensive solution is to use a DynaDisc on any chair that fits you. A DynaDisc is a flat cushion much like an exercise ball that activates your core muscles, making you sit up straight and maintain good posture. Place the DynaDisc in your chair to add height and support for your back.

DynaDisc

DESIGN WALLS

We consider design walls (also called flannel walls) to be an integral part of quiltmaking. A design wall is a vertical surface on which you can lay out and design projects. It makes it easier for you to audition fabrics for blocks, play with patterns, and work out block arrangements and spacing.

Design walls are covered with fabrics that tend to be fuzzy, allowing the blocks and quilt tops to stick to the surface without pins. Cotton flannel is the most commonly used fabric for this purpose. It can be purchased by the yard in various widths and seamed together or purchased as a bed sheet for one continuous large piece. Chamois cloth is another option; it is heavier than flannel and is available in 60″ widths. Other good design wall coverings are fleece interfacing and needle-punched cotton battings. The nap on these products tends to be thicker, making it easier to support larger pieces of fabric. Felt also works well. Any of these materials can be attached directly to the wall. You can also thumbtack it securely to the ceiling and floor to keep it from flapping. The more taut the surface, the better it will work.

Using a board that you can pin into can help when you are working with large pieces. If your design wall is attached to the wall, the space available will dictate how big the design area can be. If you don't have a large wall available, consider using a door. If a door isn't an option, you can always make a portable flannel surface. A clever idea is to take an artist's canvas, with its stretcher bar frame and taut canvas, and cover it with

flannel, using a staple gun to fix the flannel to the stretcher bars—this works great in a pinch.

Many quilters like to use foamcore board as the stabilizer for their design wall, whether that wall is portable or permanent. Foamcore comes in a variety of sizes, all the way up to 4′ × 8′. The ¼″ board tends to curl a bit, but the thicker boards are quite stable. Foamcore can be covered with flannel and leaned against any space; it can even be secured to the wall surface. Foamcore is easy to pin into, making it easy for you to position an entire quilt top on the wall. Other options in addition to foamcore include ceiling tiles, Celotex insulation board, white Styrofoam insulation (which tends to be fragile), extruded polystyrene, and builder's board (also known as Homasote). The lighter-weight boards can be left free-standing and portable, but the heavier types should be attached to the wall.

Even if you have a wall available for use as a design wall, you might also want to have a smaller, more portable design surface to work on when creating smaller projects. Compact, portable flannel surfaces are very handy to have next to your sewing machine, especially if what you're sewing is a complicated design. A 12″ × 18″ portable flannel surface is often ideal for working on one block at a time. These smaller surfaces can be of foamcore, corrugated cardboard, Masonite, and so forth—as long as the surface is sturdy enough to support the block, it will work great. They are also good for transporting blocks or units from the work wall to the sewing machine.

LIGHTING NEEDS

Lighting is one aspect that must not be overlooked in your workspace. Without proper and sufficient light, eye fatigue can constantly plague you. It can also create issues with accuracy when cutting and sewing. Whether you prefer track, fluorescent, or overhead incandescent lighting, make sure you have sufficient wattage. The type of lighting you need to create is called "task" lighting, which is functional and localized lighting for a particular activity. Task lighting is usually placed near the activity, angled to avoid glare, and distributed evenly over the work surface to minimize shadows. This type of lighting includes one or a combination of recessed, lightweight, track-mounted fixtures and shielded fluorescent tubes that either hang or are placed under shelves or cabinets.

TO PROVIDE SUFFICIENT LIGHT

❋ Don't overshield the light source. Provide just enough shading to eliminate glare.

❋ Provide adequate, but not excessive, wattage bulbs in fixtures and lamps.

❋ Lighten paint, wallpaper, carpet, and fabric colors on ceilings, walls, floors, and furnishings to obtain more light from the same wattage bulbs.

❋ Avoid glare. Direct and reflected glare cause eyestrain and discomfort.

❋ Avoid excessive contrasts of areas of light and dark. An excessive contrast in amounts of light results when one area of a room is darker than another. Correct by adding general lighting.

❋ Avoid shadows. For sewing, the source of light for a right-handed person should be on the left; for left-handed, it should be on the right.

Here is a list of helpful measurements for optimal placement of various light sources.

❋ A study lamp or high-intensity lamp by your machine should be placed 1′ to the side of the needle, 1′ above the needle, and 6″ in front of and/or behind the needle.

❋ A floor lamp should be placed to the side (approximately 15″) and slightly behind you (approximately 26″ from your lap), so light shines over your shoulder onto your project.

❋ For a table lamp, the bottom of the lampshade should be approximately 42″–44″ from the floor or at eye level for the person seated next to it.

❋ For reading and hand stitching, place a floor or table lamp in line with your shoulder and 20″ from the center of the book or project.

❋ When drafting quilt patterns or working at a desk, place a lamp 15″ to the left of your work (or to the right if you're left-handed) and 12″ toward the rear of the desk.

In Volume 3, we will give you the formula for figuring out the proper lighting output for your specific workspace.

LESSON TWO:
Adding sashing to diagonal sets

Sashing can serve two seemingly different purposes: It can separate the blocks to make each one more defined, or it can unify the blocks. If the sashing is cut from a color that contrasts highly with the colors in the blocks or if it is cut rather wide in proportion to the block size, the sashing will become a prominent design element. If the sashing is cut in a neutral color or a fabric that matches the block background and if it is cut in a width that echoes the size of the block patches, the sashing will blend in without calling attention to itself. A moderately contrasting fabric and sashing width will give you an in-between effect.

SASHING BASICS

❋ Sashing is best used when the blocks do not require a side-by-side placement for the design to flow.

❋ Sashing offers some separation for blocks that need a bit of resting space.

❋ When the sashing matches the background, it helps enhance or unify the blocks.

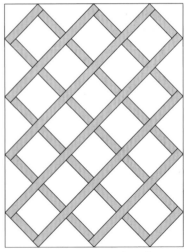

Diagonal set with simple sashing

Adding sashing with cornerstones is another option. Cornerstones are squares at the ends of sashing strips that are cut the same length as the blocks. These cornerstones bounce the eye across the quilt while unifying the blocks. The sashes separate the blocks to any degree you choose—just a little if the sashing is narrow or a great amount if it is wide. The cornerstones can be solid squares or simple pieced or appliquéd squares.

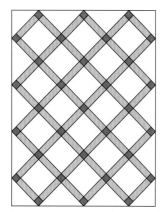

Sashing with cornerstones in diagonal set

Another idea is to let the sashing run off the edge, with the setting triangles nestled in between the sashing.

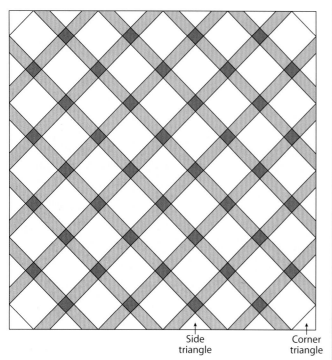

Side triangle

Corner triangle

Diagonal set with sashing that runs off the edge

To determine how wide the sashes and cornerstones should be, you should make a mock-up to study the block proportions. Many blocks include a square patch that is the grid of the block; this grid is a logical size to begin with when deciding on the width. Always leave yourself open to changing your mind about the sashing width. The fabric you choose can play a big part in the appearance of the size, not just the measurement.

We have included worksheets of each of these design ideas in Class 250 (pages 57–59) for you to play with.

tip

As a general guideline, the finished size of the sashing strip is one-fourth the size of the finished block. Using this guideline, a 6″ block would work well with a 1½″ finished sashing strip, whereas a 3″ sashing strip is often used with 12″ blocks. Remember that this is a guideline, not a rule. Let color and value play a part in your decision making.

LESSON THREE:

Figuring for setting triangles for sashed quilts

If you use sashing with your diagonal set blocks, you will need to figure your setting triangles based on the new measurements.

The setting triangles no longer equal the length of the side of the block. Instead, the side-setting triangles are now equal to the side of the block plus the finished sashing measurement. Likewise, the base of the corner triangle is equal to the side of the block plus two sashing widths. As an example, we'll use a 7″ finished block and a 1½″ finished sashing width.

SIDE TRIANGLES

METHOD A (EXACT SIZE)

7″ + 3″ (block + two 1½″ sashes) = 10″ × 1.414 = 14.14″ + 1.25″ (seam allowances) = 15.39″, rounded up to 15½″

Cut a square 15½″ and then cut it into quarters, from corner to corner.

METHOD B (FLOATING SIZES)

7″ block + 3″ for sashing × 1.414 = 14.14″ + 3″ = 17.14″ square, rounded up to 17¼″

Cut a 17¼″ square in quarters, from corner to corner.

hint

If you are confused by the different size seam allowances for triangles, just be patient with us and take our word for it. You will learn all about how this works in Volume 3.

CORNER TRIANGLES

METHOD A (EXACT SIZE)

7″ + 3″ (block + two 1½″ sashes) =
10″ ÷ 1.414 = 7.07″ + 0.875″ (seam
allowances) = 7.95″, or an 8″ square
cut in half, corner to corner

METHOD B (FLOATING SIZES)

7″ + 3″ (block + two 1½″ sashes) +
2″ = 12″ square cut in half, corner to
corner

LESSON FOUR:

Constructing the diagonal set sashed quilt

When laying out the blocks on your
design wall, be sure to insert the
sashing as you build your quilt. If you
are using a simple sashing, your strips
will be cut the length of the block.
These strips are laid between the
blocks in each row. You will also have
long strips placed between each row.

When you use sashing, you are
adding more steps to the construction of the quilt top. With careful
measuring, sewing, and pressing, your
quilt top should be straight and even
when finished.

Straight settings are a bit different
from diagonal settings when adding
sashing strips. Refer to the illustration
of simple sashing of a straight set. The
short strips, which are cut the size of
the block, are added in between each
block in each vertical row. Once the
rows are constructed, the long sashing
strips are marked and added lengthwise between each row. The final
sashing strips are then added to the
outside edges of the quilt top.

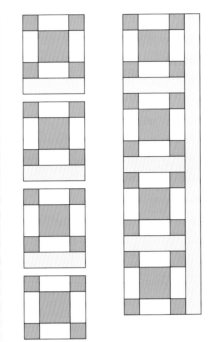

Simple sashing a straight set

The order of quilt top construction is different for diagonal sets.
Constructing this type of quilt top
can get confusing, so be sure to lay
out your blocks and sashing pieces
before you start to construct your
quilt top. Once you have laid out
the blocks on your design wall, you
will see where the sashing needs
to be placed. Study the illustration
as you read through the following
description:

For Row 1, add sashing to both sides
of the corner block. For each suc-
ceeding row, add sashing to both sides
of all the blocks. When adding the
long pieces of sashing, start with the
corner block and add a strip just to
the top of the block, measuring the
length from the outside edge of the
side sashing to the outside edge of
the opposite sashing. After the long
sash is sewn in place, add the setting
triangles to that row. For Row 2, add
a long sashing strip to the top of the
row, then add the setting triangles to
the ends of the row. For Row 3, add
a long sashing strip to the top of the

row, but then add only one setting
triangle to the left end of the row. For
Row 4, add a long sashing strip to the
top and bottom of the row. Continue
adding the long sashing strips to
the bottom of each row as you work
toward the bottom right corner.
Always add the corner triangles last.

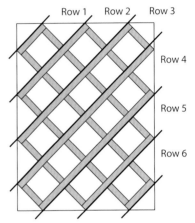

Position of sashing strips during
construction of diagonal set

As you add each length of sashing,
press the seam allowances toward
the sashing. After the rows are constructed, carefully measure the length
of each row, including the seam
allowance needed at the ends, and
cut the sashing strips to this length.
Consider cutting the strip from the
lengthwise grain, as you are more
likely to get the strip in one piece,
thereby eliminating the need for
piecing. The strip will also be less
likely to stretch when sewn along the
long length.

It is often helpful to mark placement
guides in the seam allowance of the
long, solid sashing strips. Beginning
at one end on one sash, measure the
finished size of the block plus ¼″ on
one end (for the outer seam allowance). Mark both seam allowances
or make a firm crease with an iron.
Next, measure the finished width of
the sashing and mark this distance

beyond the first mark on both edges. Then, measure the finished block again and mark. Continue down the length of the strip, ending with the finished size of a block plus ¼" on the end for the outer-edge seam allowance. Repeat this process with all the long sashing strips.

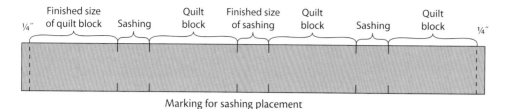

Marking for sashing placement

The strips are now ready to be sewn in between the rows. Pin the strip into position on the first row, aligning the marks to the seamlines of the blocks. Make any necessary adjustments to the sashing strip to ensure a perfect fit. Stitch the sashing to the row of blocks. Carefully press the seam allowance toward the sashing. Square the end, cutting off the excess that was added for accuracy. Continue with each row as shown for the setting you are working with until all the rows are joined.

CONSTRUCTING CORNERSTONE SASHED TOPS (BOTH STRAIGHT-SET AND DIAGONAL-SET TOPS)

Introducing cornerstones where sashing strips intersect adds a new dimension to simple sashing. Many of the techniques for measuring, cutting, and piecing will be the same as for simple sashing, but the sewing is actually easier. When cornerstones are added, no marking is needed, and each sashing strip is the same length.

1. Cut the sashing strips the same length as the unfinished blocks. The cornerstone at each corner will be the same measurement as the cut width measurement of the sashes. Cut the cornerstones. Sew the sashing strips to the blocks of each row, including the top of the first block and the bottom of the last block. Press the seams toward the sashing.

Unit placement for cornerstones

2. Construct the vertical sashing row. Sew a cornerstone to one end of a sash and then make as many squares as there are blocks in the row. Be sure that a cornerstone is at both ends of the row. Press the seams toward the sashing.

3. Sew a sashing row onto the right side of every block row, carefully butting the seams that intersect between the sashing and the cornerstone.

4. Press carefully toward the sashing. Now you're ready to join the rows. Pin the second block row onto the edge of the sashing of Row 1, carefully butting the seams as before. Check for a perfect fit and adjust as needed. If you are sashing a straight set top, once the rows are joined, add the last sashing strip to the left side of Row 1. Press toward the sashing.

LESSON FIVE:
Using sashing as a design element

Sashing strips can be pieced together using different numbers and widths of strips for different effects. Play and see what you come up with. For example, try sewing three strips together for the sashing and then add a nine-patch for the cornerstone. Another pleasing design is to sew two narrower sashing strips to either side of a wide strip, making the cornerstone a variation of the nine-patch.

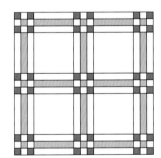

Three strips sewn together: nine-patch

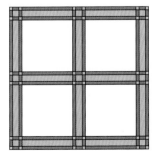

Three strips sewn together: nine-patch variation

BLOCK FRAMING (COPING STRIPS)

Block framing is the technique of sewing a strip of fabric to each side of the block. These strips can be the same fabric as the background design, or they can be a contrasting fabric. When the strips match the background, they will make the block appear to float. When contrasting fabric is used, it will emphasize the blocks.

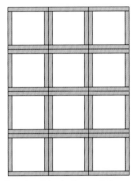

Framing blocks in straight set

Framing blocks in diagonal set

Block framing is sometimes used to standardize the size of blocks that are not all the same size. If you ever win blocks in a quilt guild block challenge, you know that the same patterns and pieces do not end up as the same size finished block (unless, of course, everyone uses the principles taught in this series of books). Strips used to standardize block size are referred to as "coping strips." To end up with blocks that are all the same size, sew an extra-wide frame around each block and then evenly square up the block. The coping strips will not all be exactly the same width when they are trimmed to size. Be careful to distribute the measurements as equally as you can from side to side and top to bottom so that it is not obvious that the block was not square in the first place.

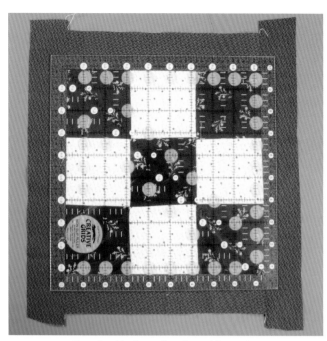

Squaring blocks to size after adding strips

Stars and Cubes—coping strips and cornerstone sashing used to make all blocks the same size

WINDOWPANING

Windowpaning is a process in which three frames are added around the block. The center strip is just ¼″ wide. The first and third strips are ½″ wide finished and can be cut from the block background fabric. The windowpane is a contrasting fabric. Windowpaning will result in perfectly straight and even ¼″ strips. Before adding strips, be sure that your block is exactly the right size square and that the corners are squared and trimmed.

Creating the strips for this technique is similar to the method used for basic borders in Volume 1, Class 180 (page 96). These strips will be cut wider than needed so that they can be trimmed down to clean up any unevenness caused by sewing over seams in the block, as well as any pressing and sewing inaccuracies.

The first round of strips will finish at ½″. Normally you would cut these strips 1″ wide (½″ finished + ½″ for seam allowances). However, for this process, cut the strips an extra ⅛″ wide, for 1⅛″ total. Stitch on opposite sides of the block, press toward the strips, and square the corners. Add the other two sides and press toward the strips. Next, measure ¾″ from the seam and trim all four sides of the block. Make sure the corners are exactly square.

Trimming and squaring first round of strips

The next strip will be the ¼″ windowpane. This strip would normally be cut ¾″ wide. However, if you ever try cutting it to this width, you will discover that once the strip is sewn in place and pressed, there is less than ½″ left and the edge is wavy. If you then try to stitch another strip to the wavy edge, the windowpane strip will not be a straight and even ¼″. Therefore, cut the windowpane strip 1″ wide.

Add windowpane strips to two sides of the block and press toward the block. Repeat for the opposite two sides. This time you will not trim the strip. You will be adding another strip to this wide strip, but measure off the seam for the ¼″ width when stitching.

Cut the third set of strips 1¼″ wide. Although you actually only need a 1″-wide strip mathematically, you have an additional bit left on the windowpane strip, and you will need that extra bit to straighten and trim the outside edge in the end. Therefore, the wider width is there to accommodate any variance.

Here is the trick to keeping the windowpane strip exactly ¼″: Align the raw edges of the windowpane strip with the third background strip. Instead of using the raw edges as a guide when sewing, you will use the left edge of your presser foot as a guide. Use your ¼″ piecing foot, or any foot that has a left toe that measures ¼″. Place the block under the foot, and align the outside edge of the left toe against the stitching, instead of the right toe against the raw edge. As you sew, keep the foot riding against the stitching the entire length of the strip, regardless of how much extra fabric is on the right side.

Position of foot against seam

Sew two opposite sides onto the block. Trim the seam allowance to ¼″ and press toward the outer strip. Square the ends of these strips. Next, add the outer strips to the remaining two sides of the block. Trim the seam allowance to ¼″ and press toward the outer strip. When you check the front of the block, you will see that the windowpaning is exactly straight and even and ¼″ wide. Trim the outer strips to ¾″ and square the corners. Now the blocks are ready to set together.

Perfect ¼″ windowpane block

Sashed quilts

PROJECT ONE: *CABIN IN THE COTTON* (WITH SIMPLE SASHING)

Cabin in the Cotton

Quilt top size: 35½″ × 47″

Grid size: 1″ (1⅝″ cut)

Block size: 7″ × 7″

Blocks: 18

Sashing width: 1″

Yardages for quilt top:

12 fat quarters (or yardage totaling 1½ yards of multiple fabrics)

1 fat quarter for center squares (or ⅛ yard)

1⅜ yards white for sashing and setting triangles

Once again, we have added a Log Cabin quilt to this book. This quilt is based on an antique quilt from the Mountain Mist collection. We have adapted the pattern to challenge your piecing skills a little. By now you have made at least two diagonal set quilts. To create this pretty little 1930s reproduction baby quilt, you will make 18 Log Cabin blocks based on a 1" grid. You will also make 10 mini Log Cabin blocks based on a ½" grid; these mini blocks will be set in the corners of your side-setting triangles. This isn't as hard as it sounds, and the results are very attractive.

This is the only quilt in this book that deals with fat quarters. As we stated earlier, for scrappy quilts, fat quarters are an easy way to work, because you can get a lot of variety using short strips (and thus smaller amounts).

This is also one of the only quilts in which you will precut all of your strips prior to sewing anything together. To figure out the yardage for this quilt, refer to Volume 1, Class 140, Lesson Four, Project 2 (page 43). The only difference between the block for this quilt and the one used in *Patriotic Log Cabin* is the size of the center square. In *Patriotic Log Cabin,* the center square was twice as wide as the logs. In *Cabin in the Cotton,* you will work with 1" center squares and 1" finished logs.

To start, prepare your fat quarters as outlined in Class 220, Lesson Three (page 20). Then cut 6 strips 1⅝" wide from each fat quarter that you have picked for the blocks, minus your center square fabric. From the fat quarter of your center square fabric, cut 2 strips 1⅝" wide and then cut these into 3 segments each. Each segment will measure approximately 1⅝" × 7".

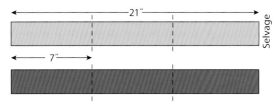

Center square fabric strips cut into segments

We want you to create this quilt quickly and efficiently. But it is a scrappy quilt, so how does that work? You are going to have organized random Log Cabin blocks because you will piece these blocks exactly as you did in Volume 1 for *Patriotic Log Cabin.* But in this quilt you will mix your short strips up a bit. So, pick one strip of each of six of your log fabrics, and set these alongside the shorter segments of the center fabric that you put aside.

Get a large basket, a brown paper bag, or a plastic box— anything that will hold all of your other log fabric strips.

Dump in your strips and mix well, but gently, and set this aside. Now it is time to start sewing.

Log fabric strips cut, mixed, and ready to sew

Making the blocks

Before you begin, make sure that your seam allowance is set correctly.

1. Sew a center fabric segment to one of the log fabrics that you set aside. You will end up with 6 different combinations sewn together. Use scissors to cut off the extra log fabric that extends a little past the center fabric strip.

Center and log fabric combinations

2. Take these strip sets to the ironing board and press the seam allowance toward the log fabric. At the cutting mat, cut these strip sets into 1½" segments. You need a total of 18 segments, so cut 3 from each strip set and set the leftovers aside for later.

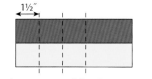

Cutting center and first log segments

3. You now have 18 centers with the first log sewn together and ready for log 2. Grab your basket, bag, or box of log fabric strips you mixed up earlier. This is where the fun starts. Pull random strips from your box and sew 2 or 3 center/log 1 segments to that strip. Be sure to align the segments on the strip so that the log fabric is feeding into your machine first, leaving about ¼″ between each segment on the strip.

Segment alignment on log 2 strip

The only "rule" when pulling out random strips is that you may not want to sew a log fabric that is the same as the previous log. Then again, you may like the effect that this gives every once in a while. It's up to you. Be creative and don't let your inner control freak take over the randomness and fun of making this quilt.

4. Once you have log 2 sewn to all 18 blocks, cut the extra strip length off each set of the segments and cut apart the segments.

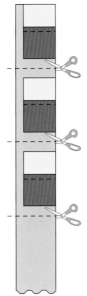

Cutting extra strip length off and segments apart

5. With the steam on, set the seam and press it toward the log you just attached. Starch your blocks (no steam).

6. At the cutting mat, trim your blocks to size: Place your ruler over the block. You will trim the center and log 1 to size first. Align the 1¼″ marking with the seam that you just sewed; trim.

Trimming blocks the first time

7. Turn the block 180° and trim the second log the same way. Turn the block 90° and trim the center square and the end of log 2, this time aligning that 1¼″ marking with the seam between the center square and log 1. Turn the block 180° again and trim the other end to 1¼″.

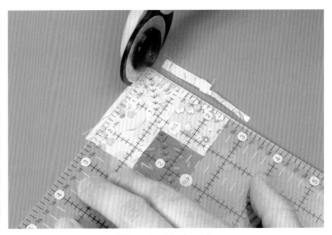

Trimming block ends

8. Once all 18 blocks are trimmed, return to the sewing machine. Pick out 6–9 more strips and repeat the sewing process to add log 3. When you align the segments on the strip to sew, *make sure that you always put the log you just sewed at the top of the strip so it feeds first into your machine.* Cut off the extra length of strip, return it to the strip box, and cut between the segments. Set your seam and press the seam allowance toward the log you just sewed on. At the cutting mat, trim the end of the log you just sewed so it is even with the center (align the 1¼″ marking with the seam between the center/log 1 unit and log 2). Once these ends are trimmed, return to your sewing machine and add log 4.

9. Once log 4 is sewn and pressed, trim these two new logs down to 1¼″. Trimming will be much easier if you use a square ruler and place the block so the two logs to be trimmed are pointed up and to the right (if you are right-handed; up and to the left if you are left-handed) as you look at the block. Align the 1¼″ marking on the top and right (or left) side seams you just sewed and trim away the excess fabric.

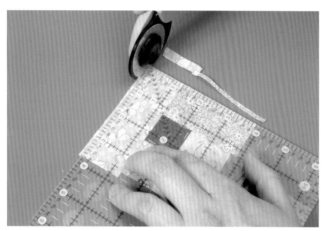
Trimming logs 3 and 4

Continue in the same manner until you have a total of 12 logs sewn onto your center squares. This will make a total of 3 log strips on each side of your block.

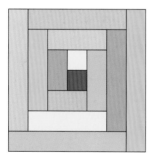
Finished *Cabin in the Cotton* block

Constructing mini blocks
Now you are ready for the mini Log Cabin blocks. Remember the little 2½″ leftover strip sets of center and log 1 fabric—you are going to use those now.

1. You are going to trim these little segments down to size for the mini blocks, sort of killing two birds with one stone. At your cutting mat, align the ⅞″ line of your ruler with the seamline and trim. Do this to both sides of the strip sets.

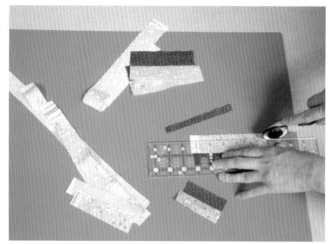
Trimming leftover strip sets down to size for mini blocks

2. Cut 2 segments 1⅛″ wide from each strip. Set these segments beside your machine. Cut 2 more strips 1⅛″ wide from your leftover fat quarters to make the mini blocks.

3. Construct the mini blocks exactly as you did the big ones. But, this time trim your logs to ¾″ from the seamline. As with the big blocks, these mini blocks will have 12 logs, with 3 logs per side.

Sashing
Now, on to sashing. Because you have one length of sashing that measures 48″ between Rows 3 and 4, you will need to work with lengthwise-grain strips. If you are wondering where this measurement comes from, refer to Class 270, Lesson Two (page 85). You can piece your sashing, but when you are working with a solid as is used in this quilt, the seams will show.

1. Measure 15″ from a selvage edge of your white fabric, make a clip on the cut/torn edge, and tear a 15″ × 49½″ strip. Take this to the ironing board, press, and starch well. Fold it in half, keeping the selvage edge together, and press the fold in. Then fold this in half one more time, again keeping that selvage edge aligned, and press. Take this piece to the cutting board to trim away the selvage edge. Then cut 9 strips each 1½″ wide.

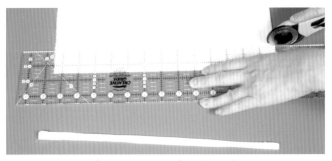

Selvage cut away and cutting strips

2. Set aside one strip. Take four strips and cut them into 24 strips, each 7½″ long.

3. Lay out these 7½″ strips and your finished large blocks on your design wall. Play with the color placement until you are happy with how your blocks look together.

4. Cut the 7 long sashing strips from the remaining 4 long strips you cut. These will be sewn between the rows. Refer to Class 270, Lesson Two (page 85) for a reminder of how to figure the length of each strip.

5. Once these sashing strips are cut to length, lay them out between your rows of blocks. You are now ready to construct your setting triangles using your mini Log Cabin blocks.

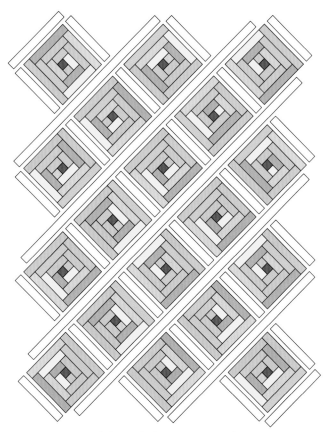

Quilt layout before setting triangles

Setting triangles

This quilt has rather deceiving side-setting triangles. They are the size of the large blocks in the quilt but have the little mini block added in the corner. To make these side-setting triangles, use the finished size of the mini blocks to determine the size your triangles will be. The mini blocks should be 4″ (this includes your seam allowance), so they will finish at 3½″. Now, use the formula you learned in Class 230, Lesson Two (page 23):

3.5″ × 1.414 = 4.95″, rounded up to 5″

5″ + 3″ = 8″

You need 20 triangles. You get four triangles per square, which means you need 5 – 8″ squares:

5 × 8″ = 40″, or one strip cut 8″ wide

Once you have your triangles cut, sew one triangle to the left side of all 10 mini Log Cabin blocks.

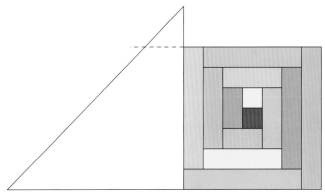

Adding and trimming first triangle to mini Log Cabin blocks

Press the seam allowance toward the triangle. Trim the point extending beyond the block so it is even with the block.

Sew the other triangle to the right side of the corner of the mini blocks and press toward the triangle. Add these to your quilt layout on your design wall.

Next, you will need to determine the size of your corner triangles and then cut the fabric. For floating triangles, you will take the straight measurement of your block (7″), add the width of the 2 sashing strips (1½″ each), and then add 2″ to that measurement:

7″ + 3″ + 2″ = 12″

You have 4 corner triangles, so you need 2 squares cut in half diagonally.

Add these triangles to your quilt on the wall.

Complete quilt layout

PROJECT TWO: *FOUR-PATCH LATTICE*

Four-Patch Lattice

You are now ready to construct your quilt. Start by sewing the block-size sashing strips to the blocks. Press these seams toward the sashing strips.

Next, add the setting triangles to the ends of each row. Once the rows are constructed, you can start to add the long sashing strips to the tops (or bottoms) of each row, again pressing the seams toward the sashing. Sew the rows together until you have two halves of your quilt. Finally, sew the two halves together and add the corner triangles to complete your quilt.

Quilt top size: 52½″ × 65″

Grid size: 2″

Block size: 8″ × 8″

Blocks: 32

Sashing width: 1″

Yardages for quilt top:

⅞ yard black

⅝ yard peach

⅝ yard red

¾ yard light green for sashing

⅛ yard dark green for cornerstones

1⅓ yards large print

Making the blocks

FOUR-PATCH BLOCKS

Formula: 32 blocks, 2 four-patches per block, 2 segments per four-patch:

$32 \times 2 = 64 \times 2 = 128$ segments

The grid for this quilt is 2″ finished, or 2½″ cut:

$128 \times 2.5″ = 320″ \div 42″ = 7.62$, or 8 strips

Cut:

8 strips 2½″ wide of the peach

8 strips 2½″ wide of the red

1. To construct the four-patches, sew 8 strip sets of the peach and red together. Press and starch the seam allowance toward the red strip. Measure each strip to make sure each measures 2¼″ from the seam to the raw edge. Trim if necessary. From these strip sets, cut 128 segments 2½″ wide.

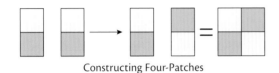

Constructing Four-Patches

2. Make two stacks of segments, one turned the opposite direction of the other so that you have a checkerboard effect. The stack on the right should have the red square on top so that the seam allowance raw edge feeds into the machine first.

3. Start sewing by placing one unit from the stack on the right (stack 2) on top of one unit from the stack on the left (stack 1), right sides together. Chain sew until all 64 four-patches are joined. Fan the seams of your four-patches, then press and starch. Measure to be sure that your units are exactly 4½″ square.

> *note* For a refresher on how to fan your seam allowances, refer to Volume 1, Class 150, Lesson Six (page 58).

Now, you need to cut the black fabric strips that make up the other half of your double Four-Patch block.

DOUBLE FOUR-PATCH BLOCKS

Formula: 32 blocks × 2 black squares per block = 64 segments

This square is the same size as your completed four-patch units:

64 × 4.5″ = 288″ ÷ 42″ = 6.86, or 7 strips

Cut:

7 strips 4½″ wide of the black

Construct these units using the same method used when constructing *Town Square* in Volume 1, Class 150 (page 65). With the black strip facing up, position a four-patch on top, right sides together. *Always have the red square of the four-patch at the top right corner.*

1. Stitch the right side of the block/strip unit together. Leave ¼″ of space between each four-patch as you place them on the black strip and sew them together. Continue until you have all 64 four-patch units attached to the black strips.

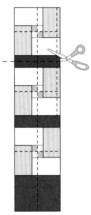

Four-patch units being sewn onto black strip

2. Use scissors to cut between the units in the ¼″ space you created in Step 1. Press the seam allowance toward the black square; starch. At the cutting mat, align your ruler with the seams and the cut edge of the four-patch. Cut the black strip so it is exactly 4½″ wide from top to bottom and 4¼″ from the seam.

3. Assemble these units just as you did for your small four-patch. Create two stacks of 32 units each. Turn one stack the opposite direction of the other so that you have a checkerboard effect. Your right-hand stack will have the black block on top so that the seam allowance raw edge feeds into the machine first. Take one unit from stack 2 (the right-hand stack) and place it right sides together with a unit from stack 1. Butt the seams and chain sew your blocks together. Fan your seams, press, and starch your blocks.

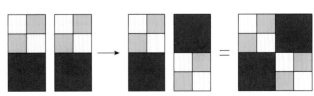

Creating double Four-Patch block

SASHING, CORNERSTONES, AND SETTING TRIANGLES

Now it is time to cut your sashing, cornerstones, and setting triangles. Refer to the following quilt illustration.

Start by counting the number of light green sashing strips and cornerstones you'll need. Did you come up with 80 sashing strips and 49 cornerstones? Great!

How many side-setting triangles? 14!

Formula: 80 sashing strips × 8½″ long (by 1½″ wide): 80 × 8.5″ = 680″ ÷ 42″ = 16.19, or 17 strips

Formula: 49 cornerstones × 1½″ square (cut) = 73.5″ ÷ 42″ = 1.75, or 2 strips

Formula: 14 side triangles ÷ 4 = 3.5, or 4 squares

To figure the size, remember the two-part formula from Lesson Three (page 38):

(# of blocks per row × size of block) + (# of sashing strips per row × width of sashing)

This formula gives the straight measurement needed to continue figuring the yardage for the side-setting and corner triangles.

Let's use the very first row with only one block in it:

(1 block × 8″) + (2 sashings × 1″ wide) = 8″ + 2″ = 10″ × 1.414 = 14.14 + 3″ = 17.14″

In ruler language this is 17¼″. You need four of these squares.

Your fabric width is only 42″, or 42″ ÷ 17″ = 2.47. In this case, we will round down, because you can only get two usable size squares from one fabric strip.

For the corner triangles, you need two squares. Again, the width of the block plus the sashing equals 10″; add 2″ to this to find that you need to cut 2 – 12″ squares for your corner triangles.

Cut:

    17 strips 1½″ wide of the light green

    2 strips 1½″ wide of the dark green

    2 strips 17¼″ wide of the large print

    1 strip 12″ wide of the large print

Subcut the light green strips into 8½″ lengths and the dark green into 1½″ lengths. Go ahead and cut your 4 – 17¼″ squares and 2 – 12″ squares for your side-setting and corner triangles and subcut them diagonally.

Now you are ready to go to your design wall and lay out your quilt.

Quilt layout

Assembling the quilt top

You will now construct your long sashing strips, starting with the row on the top left corner. This row is made up of a cornerstone, a sashing strip, and another cornerstone. Pick up these pieces in that order, take them to your sewing machine, and sew the cornerstones onto both ends of the sashing. Press toward the sashing strip and starch.

Continue in this manner, picking up the cornerstones and sashing strips of each row in order and piecing them together. Always press your seam allowance toward the light green.

Once you have constructed all the sashing rows, you need to sew the sashing strips and side-setting triangles in the block rows onto the blocks. This is the same thing you did for *Cabin in the Cotton* (page 46). Again, always press the seam allowance toward the light green. Trim the points of the side-setting triangles so they are flush with the top of the cut edge of your blocks and sashing.

Once all the block rows are joined, you can assemble your quilt in halves, then join the halves, and finally add the corner triangles.

And you have made another pretty quilt top! Good job!

PROJECT THREE: *CARD TRICK*

Card Trick

Quilt top size: 36″ × 48″

Grid size: 1½″

Block size: 6″ × 6″ + windowpaning

Blocks: 18

Yardages for quilt top:

2⅝ yards cream

⅛ yard red

⅛ yard green

⅛ yard blue

⅝ yard brown

YUMs

If you have been following along with us since Volume 1, you will recognize that this is a combined grid quilt. If you are new to this series, however, you need to know about YUMs. YUM is our acronym for **Y**our **U**nique **M**easurement, which we introduced in the *Inlaid Tile* table runner (Volume 1, Class 170, Lesson Four, page 85). YUMs are necessary in quilts in which you measure from one seam allowance to another on one part of a block or quilt to determine the exact cut size of another part of the block or quilt so that you end up with a perfectly square block. We do this with combined grids so that you do not have to stretch or ease things to make them fit.

For the fun blocks in this quilt, you have only two configurations of strip sets in two colorways each.

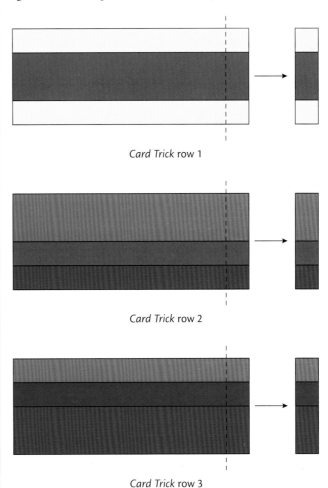

Card Trick row 1

Card Trick row 2

Card Trick row 3

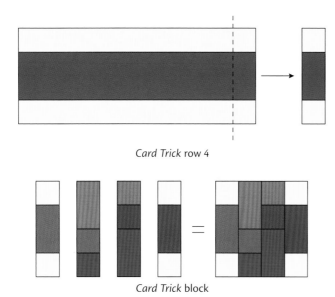

Card Trick row 4

Card Trick block

To make enough strip sets for 18 blocks, you need 18 segments 2″ wide: 18 × 2″ = 36″, which is less than one whole strip each.

Before you precut all the strips to make the strip sets, let's focus on constructing combined grids. In order to have the parts of the block that are a combined grid come out to the exact size, you need to cut and construct strips that are the size of the grid (the smallest) and then measure those for your sizing. Then, if you have multiple combined grids, you need to cut your next widest strip to that size and sew it, and so on. If you are confused, refer to Volume 1, Class 170, Lesson Four (page 80), and the three quilts in that Class. If you haven't already made any of these quilts, give them a shot!

For this lesson, things are a little easier and more straightforward. *Card Trick* has only one combined grid.

So, with the explanation out of the way, the best way to learn is by doing. Off we go!

Constructing the strip sets

Rows 2 and 3 contain the combined grid unit. So we will start by making these rows first.

1. Cut the narrow strips for Rows 2 and 3 first. You need 1 strip 2″ wide each of blue, brown, green, and red. Lay out the strips so that they match the illustration above. Sew the 2 strips of each strip set together.

2. Press the seams toward the blue fabric in Row 2 and the red fabric in Row 3. At the cutting table, measure from the seamline to ensure that the strips are now 1¾″ wide; trim as needed.

3. Now combined grids come into play. The measurement of the wide strip should be exactly the same as the measurement of the two narrow strips sewn together. If you were not accurate with your cutting or sewing, you can compensate for size discrepancy by working with YUM. Once you have determined the size of the 2 narrow strips sewn together, cut the 2 wider strips to that measurement (mathematically correct would be 3½″).

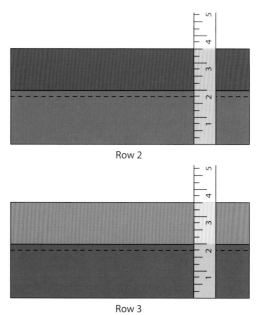

Row 2

Row 3

Measuring back side of strips to determine measurement for next strip

4. Sew the red strip to the brown fabric of Row 2 and the blue strip to the green fabric of Row 3. For Row 2, press toward the brown, and for Row 3, press toward the green. Again, for accuracy, measure from the seam. The new strip should measure 3¼″; trim to this width if necessary (or ¼″ smaller than YUM).

5. Now you're ready to sew the strip sets for Rows 1 and 4. For each row, you need 2 strips of cream cut 2″ wide. You also need a 3½″-wide strip (or YUM) of brown and green for Rows 1 and 4, respectively. Sew one cream strip to one side of each colored strip. Press the seam allowance toward the colored strip. At the cutting table, measure from the seam for both strips; the cream strips should be 1¾″, and the colored strips should be 3¼″. Trim if necessary.

6. To complete your strip sets, add the final cream strip to the other side of the colored strips in Rows 1 and 4. Press toward the colored strip and measure. Trim the cream strips if necessary.

Making the blocks

1. From each strip set, cut 18 segments 2″ wide. Place the stacks of segments to the right of your sewing machine in the order shown in the block illustration on page 52. Row 1 on the left, then Row 2 to the right of that, and so on.

2. Sew Rows 2 and 3 together first, making sure that the center seams butt perfectly. Before you press, fan the center seam to eliminate the bulkiness of all the seams coming together and to alleviate any distortion caused by the seam allowances of the other row being pressed over onto the wider pieces.

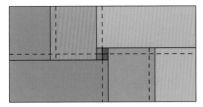

Fanning seam between Rows 2 and 3

3. Press the seam allowances in the appropriate direction according to the fanned seam; starch lightly. Take these partial blocks to the cutting table and measure from the seamline. Each row segment should measure 1¾″. Trim off any excess.

4. Add Row 1 to the Row 2 side of the blocks. Press the seam allowances open to reduce bulk; starch and trim the Row 1 segment as before.

5. Add the Row 4 segments. Press the seams open, starch, and trim.

That's it … that easy. Now it is time to add the windowpaning to really set off the blocks. Follow the instructions for creating windowpaning (page 42) to complete your blocks. Then, come back here and we will continue with laying out your quilt, adding the setting triangles, and constructing your quilt top.

Setting triangles

Card Trick has 10 side triangles ÷ 4 = 2.5, or 3 squares needed. To figure the size, this time you will figure the setting triangles the normal way, as sashing was not used.

When you add windowpaning, the "sashing" is built into the block. Measure the side of the block (6″ + 1.25 + 1.25 = 8.5″) × 1.414 + 3″. What size square do you need? You need three 15″ squares. Your width of fabric is only 42″, or 42 ÷ 15 = 2.8. In this case, we will round down because you can only get two usable-size squares from one strip of fabric. Cut 2 – 15″ strips.

For the corner triangles, you need two squares. Again, the finished width of the block plus the sashing equals 8½″. Add 2″ to this and you now know you need to cut two 10½″ squares for your corner triangles. Cut the side-setting triangles in fourths diagonally and the corner triangles in half diagonally.

> **note** *If you want to challenge yourself, try making the setting triangles with the strip in them as Carrie did. You will find the instructions for how to do this in Class 280, Lesson Three (page 98).*

Now you are ready to go to your design wall, lay out your quilt, and start the assembly process. Have fun!

Card Trick quilt layout

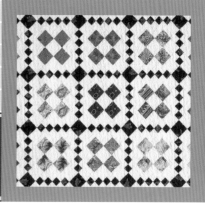

Class 250

LESSON ONE:

Planning simple diagonal sets

One of the most useful tools for designing a diagonal set quilt is diagonal graph paper (see Resources, page 112). This Class includes several worksheets for you to work with that will make designing and planning your quilts more fun. Whether you are doing a simple diagonal set or one with linking blocks and internal frames, drawing the idea on paper will benefit you in the planning process.

In Volume 1, Class 150 (pages 50–56), we discussed planning a simple straight set quilt. This was a fairly easy task—once you know what size you want your quilt to be and know the size of the design block, a simple matter of division takes place and things take shape quickly. This is not the case with diagonal sets. Diagonal sets are a visual maze, with inside rows, outside rows, setting triangles, and corners. Then add in sashing, and you really have to see it to understand it.

THE WORKSHEETS

This Class includes nine worksheets:

1. Simple diagonal set (side by side blocks)

2. Alternate blocks (use as either plain or pieced alternate blocks) in a diagonal set

3. Simple sashing

4. Sashing with setting squares

5. Sashing that runs off the edge

6. Framed blocks in a diagonal set

7. Framed blocks with windowpaning in a diagonal set

8. Zigzag set (covered in Class 260, Lesson Four, page 76)

9. Bar set (covered in Class 260, Lesson Three, page 75)

These design elements will be discussed in detail later in Class 260. For now, we want to address how to plan the size of the quilt using a diagonal setting.

The worksheets included here are the basic skeletons of the various layouts for each setting. We suggest that you photocopy these sheets for drawing and coloring in your own designs. Once you start inserting different blocks and combinations into the worksheets, you are likely to become addicted to the design phase of planning a quilt. Keep your worksheets in a notebook for future reference and ideas.

PLANNING YOUR QUILTS USING THE WORKSHEETS

Creating a scale drawing of a quilt allows you to see what the quilt will look like before you start to cut and sew your fabric. You can play with colors and values, textures and shades to see how they all work together. Once the line drawings are done, you can mock up the drawing using actual fabrics, as will be discussed in Lesson Two (page 64). From this drawing, you can learn a great deal about your likes and dislikes, while also giving yourself an opportunity to experiment with various design elements.

The worksheets are laid out in a square format. If you want to design a quilt top that is longer than it is wide, simply adapt the drawing by adding as many extra rows as needed. Make photocopies of the worksheet, cut them apart, and tape them together to the size you desire.

When you start to draft the blocks that will fit into the worksheet, consider the scale of the graph paper. Graph paper is available in different numbers of squares per inch. The most common are ¼″ and ⅛″ scale. Try to have on hand several different scales of graph paper (see Resources, page 112).

The worksheets in this Class are 1″ square, so we suggest that you draw your blocks to fit that area. To draw each block as a 1″ square, select graph paper that relates to your chosen block in its seam divisions (grid). Most blocks have equal grid divisions. Once you determine what the grid is, you will find it easy to draw the block. The graph paper pack available for this book (see Resources, page 112) has 3, 4, 5, 6, 7, 8, 9, and 10 squares-per-inch paper. The different grids make working with the block grid easy. If you know the base grid of your block, simply use the same number of squares as in the grid of the block. For example, if you have a Seven-Patch block, use 7-to-the-inch graph paper. If you have a Five-Patch block, but each grid is subdivided, use 10-to-the-inch graph paper. Once the blocks are drawn out to be 1″ square, they will fit into the worksheet squares.

Example of simple diagonal set

Simple diagonal set

Sashing with cornerstones

Example of sashing with cornerstones

Sashing that runs off the edge

Example of sashing that runs off the edge

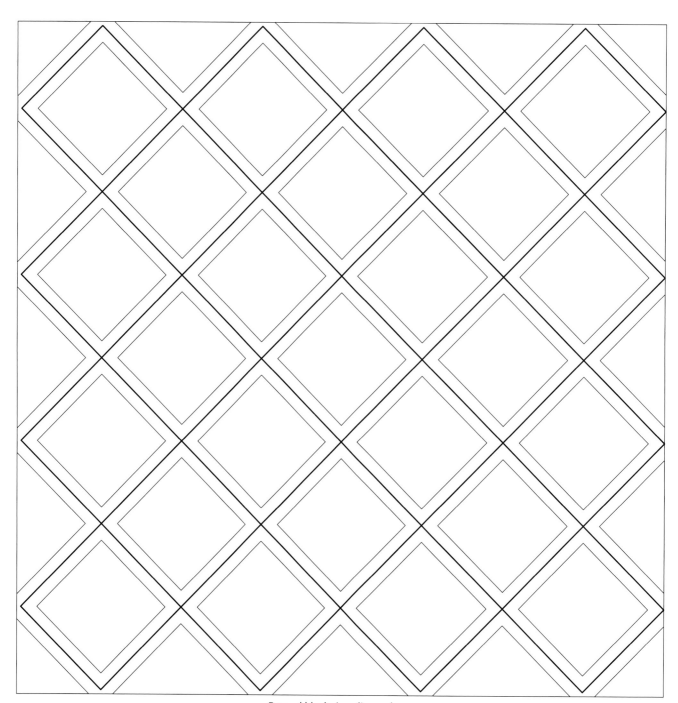

Framed blocks in a diagonal set

Example of framed blocks in a diagonal set

Framed blocks with windowpaning in a diagonal set

Example of framed blocks with
windowpaning in a diagonal set

Zigzag set

Example of zigzag set

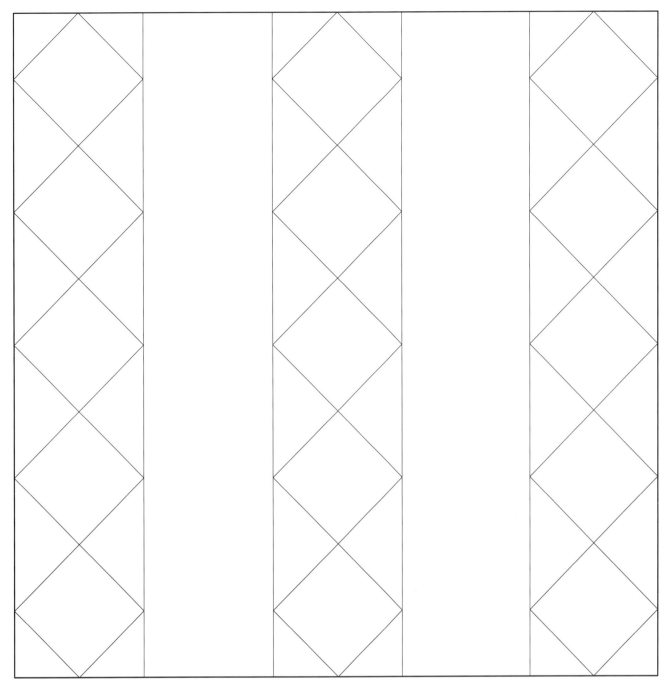

Bar set

Example of bar set

LESSON TWO:
Figuring the quilt size

As you draw the blocks on the graph paper, be sure to take into account the scale. One square of the graph paper can represent ¾″, 1″, 1½″, 2″, or any size you want. Whatever size you choose, the scale *must* be consistent within the drawing. Note the scale you are working with so that you can stay consistent with the sashing and alternate blocks. Do not change the scale within the design. Once you have drawn the blocks, you can use your scale to figure the finished quilt size.

If you are designing a straight set quilt, simply add up the total number of graph paper squares and multiply by the scale you have chosen.

Example: If one square on the graph paper equals 1″ of the quilt and the quilt drawing is 90 squares wide × 108 squares long, the finished quilt would be 90″ × 108″.

Working with diagonal set quilts is a bit different. Because the squares of the graph paper are on-point, you cannot simply count the squares to determine the finished quilt size. You will need to go an extra step and multiply the finished size of the block by 1.414. The diagonal of any square is always 1.414 times longer than the sides of the square.

Example: There are five squares in each block. You have assigned a scale of 1½″ per square, which means the block finishes at 7½″. The diagonal measurement of 7½″ is 7.5″ × 1.414 = 10.6″. If you have planned 9 blocks wide and 11 blocks long, you would multiply 9 × 10.6″ = 95.4″ and 11 × 10.6″ = 116.6″. But these measurements are a bit larger than you might like the quilt to be. What if you changed the scale of the block to 1¼″? That would make the block finish at 6¼″: 6.25″ × 1.414 = 8.84″ × 9 blocks = 79.5″. If you add a block to the row, you would have 10 blocks × 8.84″ = 88.4″. This is close to the 90″ measurement you want. If you add another row to the length of the quilt (12 × 8.84″ = 106″), you are almost at 108″. You could also try making the scale of the block larger, which would make it fewer blocks wide and long. As you can see, working with the numbers lets you design a quilt the size you desire.

If all this seems like too much work for you, the chart shown here might be of help. If you know what size you want your block to be, read across the first row to find the block size. Look at the second row to find the diagonal measurement, rounded up or down as appropriate. The rows below this measurement tell you the diagonal measurement of multiple blocks point-to-point across the width or length of the quilt. For example, if you have designed a quilt with 9″ blocks, and the layout is five blocks across and seven blocks down, the quilt would be 63¾″ × 89¼″.

Once you have designed the body of the quilt top, you can determine how much space is left for additional borders if desired.

Block Sizes and Their Diagonal Measurements

Straight Block Size	6″	7½″	8″	9″	10″	12″
1 Block on diagonal	8½″	10½″	11¼″	12¾″	14″	17″
2 Blocks	17″	21″	22½″	25½″	28″	34″
3 Blocks	25½″	31½″	33¾″	38¼″	42″	51″
4 Blocks	34″	42″	45″	51″	56″	68″
5 Blocks	42½″	52½″	56¼″	63¾″	70″	85″
6 Blocks	51″	63″	67½″	76½″	84″	102″
7 Blocks	59½″	73½″	78¾″	89¼″	98″	119″
8 Blocks	68″	84″	90″	102″	112″	
9 Blocks	76½″	94½″	101¼″	114¾″		
10 Blocks	85″	105″	112½″			
11 Blocks	93½″	115½″				
12 Blocks	102″					

LESSON THREE:
Alternate blocks

Nothing seems to create excitement for a quilt block like putting it on-point. Class 230 (page 22) introduced the simple diagonal set, and Class 240 (page 37) introduced using sashing to separate blocks. However, not all blocks can hold their own when placed side by side; the different units may run together, and the overall pattern can become lost in the confusion. Likewise, if you audition sashing between the blocks, it may break up an existing pattern or cause the quilt to look unbalanced.

This lesson will introduce you to creating space between the blocks by adding alternate, or linking, blocks between the pieced blocks.

PLAIN ALTERNATE BLOCKS

Alternating solid squares with the design blocks can make the quilt top look very different. Solid squares can provide blank space where a lot of quilting or a wonderful large-scale fabric can be showcased. Using a plain block that is the same as the background of the pieced block can connect the block patterns into a chain at the corners, creating a floating look for the design. Plain alternate blocks also help you make the most of a limited number of pieced blocks. *Nine-Patch on Point* (made in Class 230, page 29) is an example of a plain alternate block in a diagonal set. Use Worksheet 2 to design alternate block sets.

Diagonal set with plain alternate blocks

LINKING OR CONNECTING BLOCKS

The alternate block can also be pieced. These pieced blocks separate and connect the design blocks. If the pieced alternate block creates a secondary design with the design block, it is often referred to as a connecting, or linking, block. Linking blocks often create interesting variations, or even a secondary design, when combined in an alternating pattern with different pieced blocks. Once all the blocks are joined in a design, it is often difficult to find the individual blocks that make up the pattern.

A linking block plays directly off the design of the primary design block. It is helpful to base both the design block and the linking block on the same grid. Linking blocks also help beginning quilters achieve a look of difficulty without the piecing getting difficult.

Following are various blocks that work well as linking blocks. Several have triangles, which really add a lot of excitement. Play with blocks with triangles so that you start to get excited about Volume 3, which is entirely devoted to triangle techniques and quilts.

The first group of blocks shown here includes typical blocks used in design; these blocks may not create a secondary design. All of these blocks, which are scaled to 1″ to fit the worksheets, can be redrafted to different grids as needed. Just photocopy them or draw them in multiples and place them between design blocks of your choice. You will probably get hooked on the process, as the ideas are limitless once you get started.

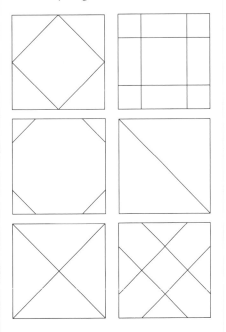

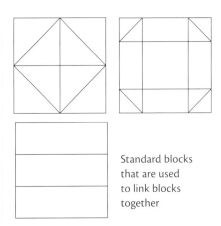

Standard blocks that are used to link blocks together

A linking block can be a simple pieced square that serves as a simple companion block for a more complex block design. Substituting a simple pieced block for a plain alternate block creates some interesting and attractive variations. If the linking block has a similar division of space as the design block, an overall feeling of depth and movement evolves. A good way to identify linking blocks is to see if the two blocks share corners—this is where the designs of both blocks meet at the corners and complete the total design. The most obvious of these is the *Double Irish Chain* you made in Volume 1 (page 87). The simple Five-Patch block alternates with a simpler linking block to create a very pleasing diagonal chain. These linking blocks work for both straight sets and diagonal sets. Compare the illustrations of the *Double Irish Chain* (straight set) with that of the *Five-Patch Chain* (diagonal set). They are both made of the same pieced units, but the setting completely changes the appearance of the quilt top.

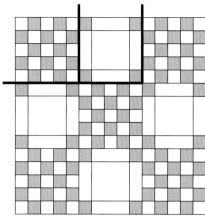

Double Irish Chain—straight set

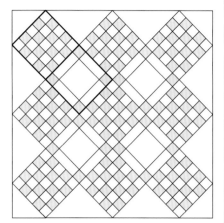

Five-Patch Chain—diagonal set

A new overall pattern does not always result. A simple linking block can add interest and secondary designs without playing directly off the original block. It's a fun way to add interest to simple blocks. It also allows you to make a quilt larger without adding more of the complex original blocks.

Adding a linking block for interest

More elaborate linking blocks can create exciting secondary designs when paired with pieced design blocks. The more complex the piecing in both blocks, the more exciting the quilt top can be.

This group of illustrations represents more elaborate blocks. Use them in the same way as you used the simpler linking blocks and have fun playing with them to create original designs.

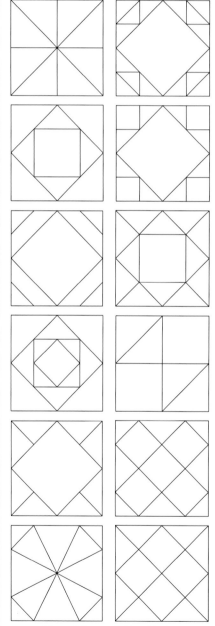

More elaborate linking blocks

Design with complex linking block

These blocks are used specifically to make chains.

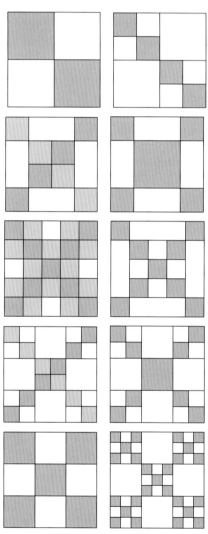

Linking blocks used to make chains

Design with chain surrounding block

A fun and exciting way to work is to take different design blocks and draw them on graph paper, using any of the linking blocks as alternating blocks. Use the worksheets in this Class to position your blocks. Photocopy the worksheets so that you can try several different ideas. Once you have selected a design block, draw it on graph paper, photocopy it several times, and place the copies in the squares that are shown as shaded. If the design block you chose is complex, a simpler block that echoes its lines might be the perfect choice to extend some lines and connect the design overall.

As you play, notice how much interaction occurs between the two different blocks. Does a secondary design emerge? Work with an arrangement of at least 3 blocks × 3 blocks of each combination. Don't forget that color placement can really play a role when working with these blocks.

Experiment with different linking blocks in the blank square. Draw any blocks or simple lines of your choice. Keep playing until you find the combination that makes you want to sew!

LESSON FOUR:

The quilts

PROJECT ONE: FIVE-PATCH CHAIN

This is simply a Double Irish Chain on-point with a contrasting color for the side-setting triangles. You will notice if you compare this version to a traditional Irish Chain that the color placement is different (see Volume 1, Class 170, page 87). This is because the corners of the B block being stronger than the corners of the A block. For detailed instructions on construction of and figuring strip sets, refer to Volume 1, Class 170 (page 82).

Quilt top size: 66″ × 66″

Grid size: 1¾″

Block size: 8¾″

Blocks:

25 A blocks

16 B blocks

16 side-setting triangles

4 corner triangles

Yardages for quilt top:

1¾ yards cream

1⅜ yards brown dot

1⅛ yards pink

1⅜ yards dark brown print

Five-Patch Chain

Making Block A

For Rows 1 and 5, you need 3 strip sets. Cut 6 strips each of brown dot and cream and 3 strips of pink; cut each 2¼″ wide.

For Rows 2 and 4, you need 3 strip sets. Cut 6 strips of pink and 9 strips of brown dot; cut each 2¼″ wide.

For Row 3, you need 1½ strip sets. Cut 5 strips of pink and 3 strips of brown dot; cut each 2¼″ wide.

1. Cut the strips, lay them out in the order of the rows, and start sewing them together. For Rows 1 and 5 and Rows 2 and 4, you will construct 3 strip sets each. For Row 3, you will need 1½ strip sets. Press all the strips toward the brown dot; starch. Remember to trim the strips to the correct width after adding each one. Each strip should measure 2″ from the seam to the raw edge.

2. Cut the strip sets into 2¼″ segments. You need:

50 segments from the Row 1 and 5 strip set

50 segments from the Row 2 and 4 strip set

25 segments from the Row 3 strip set

Make stacks for each row from the segments.

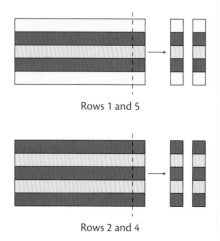

Rows 1 and 5

Rows 2 and 4

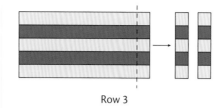

Row 3

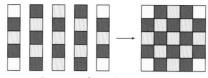

Segments for making Block A

3. To assemble, transfer the stacks to the right side of your sewing machine. Start with Row 1 and Row 2 (2 on top of 1), butting the seams carefully. Chain sew the units.

4. Fan all the seam allowances. Starch and measure for accuracy, trimming if necessary.

5. Add Row 3 and fan the seams. Press, starch, and measure.

6. Add Row 4. Fan the seams, press, starch, and measure.

7. Finally, add Row 5 and fan all the seams. Press, starch, and trim.

Back of block with all seams fanned

The blocks should all measure exactly 9¼″ square, from raw edge to raw edge. Check each block and correct if necessary.

Turn over the block and measure from raw edge to raw edge, from the brown dot square in Row 1 to the raw edge of the other brown dot square. Hold open the seam allowances as you do this. The mathematical measurement should be 5¼″. How close are you?

Do you remember the YUM (Your Unique Measurement) idea we presented in Volume 1 (page 85)? This is where different blocks that work with different units join. The measurements need to be exact, even though the units are combined on one block and sewn on the other. The combined grid measurement for this block is 5¼″ or YUM. This is the measurement to cut the wide strip of cream for Rows 1 and 3 in Block B. It is also the measurement of the center square for Block B.

Measuring for YUM for Block B

If your measurement is anything other than 5¼″, your personal measurement will be what you use to cut these units.

Making Block B

For Rows 1 and 3, you need 2 strip sets. Cut 4 strips of dark brown 2¼″ wide and 2 strips of cream 5¾″ (or YUM) wide.

For Row 2, you will need 2½″ strip sets. Cut 5 strips of cream 2¼″ wide and 3 strips of cream 5¾″ (or YUM) wide.

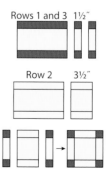

Rows 1 and 3   1½″

Row 2   3½″

1. Sew the strip sets together as you did for Block A. Press (see note), starch, and (if necessary) trim the strips.

2. Once the strip sets have been assembled, cut the Row 1 and 3 strip sets into 32 segments each 2¼″ wide. Cut Row 2 into 16 segments each 5¾″ wide.

3. Make stacks of the rows and sew these together—Row 2 to Row 1. Press, starch, and trim if necessary.

4. Sew Row 3 to Row 2 and press, starch, and measure for accuracy. When these blocks are finished, they too should measure exactly 9¼″ square. When you lay Block A next to Block B, the seams of Rows 1 and 5 of Block A should match perfectly to the seams of Rows 1 and 3 of Block B.

Assembling the quilt top

It is time to lay out the blocks into a diagonal set on your design wall. Refer to the illustration to create five rows of five blocks each of Block A on-point. Place the B blocks in between them.

SIDE-SETTING TRIANGLES

To figure the size needed for the side-setting triangles, measure Block A from corner to corner, and subtract ½″ for seam allowance. The block is 8¾″ square, $8.75″ \times 1.414 = 12.37″ = 12.5″ + 3″ = 15.5″$, which is the size you need to cut the squares for the side-setting triangles.

You need 12 side-setting triangles, and you get four from each 15½″ square. Therefore, you need to cut 4 – 15½″ squares of the dark brown print. Cut these squares in half both directions diagonally. Position the triangles on the design wall at the ends of the rows.

CORNERS

For the corners, add 2″ to the 8¾″ measurement of the block. Cut 2 – 11″ squares and cut them in half diagonally. Position the corners on the design wall.

Sew the rows together and add the side-setting triangles to the ends of each row. Press the seam allowance of each row before adding another row. Construct half of the top; then construct the second half. Once the halves are joined, add the corners.

Do not trim the edges until the quilt top is quilted. If you want to add any additional borders, refer to Class 280 (page 96) for squaring the top before adding borders.

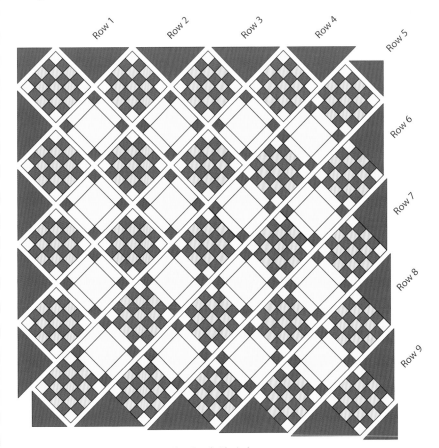

Five-Patch Chain layout

This quilt is typically set in a straight set, but oh how striking when placed on the diagonal! This can be very scrappy, with the chain blocks one color as pictured, or it can be much more controlled if you don't want the scrappy look. Play with color and have fun with this one!

Quilt top size: 52″ × 61″

Grid size: 1″ (Four-Patch block)

Block size: 6″

Blocks:

    42 Chain blocks

    30 Nine-Patch blocks

Yardages for quilt top:

    1⅔ yards white

    ¾ yard blue

    30 – ¼-yard pieces or fat quarters

The construction of both blocks in this quilt is quite simple. The connector block, which is made up of four-patches set in a nine-patch set, will be constructed first because it has the smallest units.

Four-Patch Chain on-point, designed by Janice Benight

Making the connector block

Let's review the math involved in figuring out the number of strip sets and strips to cut.

You need 168 four-patch units (42 blocks × 4 four-patches per block). Each four-patch uses 2 segments, and each segment is cut to 1½″:

168 × 2 = 336 segments × 1.5″ = 504″ ÷ 42″ = 12 strip sets

Cut 12 strips 1½″ wide of blue and 12 strips 1½″ wide of white.

You also need 2 – 2½″ squares for Rows 1 and 3 to go between the four-patch units:

42 blocks × 2 = 84 × 2.5″ = 210″ ÷ 42″ = 5 strips of white, 2½″ wide

Subcut strips into 84 – 2½″ squares

For Row 2, you need 1 segment per block:

42 × 1 = 42 segments × 2.5″ = 105″ ÷ 42″ = 2.5 strip sets

Cut 5 strips 2½″ wide of white and 3 strips 2½″ wide of blue.

Note: You will only use half of the third blue strip.

Totals to cut:

    12 strips 1½″ wide of blue

    12 strips 1½″ wide of white

    10 strips 2½″ wide of white

    3 strips 2½″ wide of blue

Starting with the four-patch units, sew 12 strip sets using the 1½″ blue and white strips. Press the seams toward the blue strip, starch, and measure to be sure that each strip is exactly 1¼″ from the seam to the raw edge. Cut 336 segments 1½″ wide from the strip sets.

Four-patch strip set progression

Make two equal stacks of the four-patch segments, with one stack turned the opposite direction from the other so that you have a checkerboard effect. The stack on the right should have the blue square on top so that the seam allowance raw edge leads into the machine. Begin sewing by placing one unit from stack 2 on top of one unit from stack 1 (remember, two on top of one), and chain sew until all 168 pairs are joined. Remember that the blue square should *always* be at the top as it goes into the machine. Fan the seams and then press and starch if necessary, and measure to make sure that the units are exactly 2½″ square.

> *note* If you are unsure about chain sewing the four-patches, refer to Volume 1, Class 150, Lesson Six (pages 57–58) for detailed instructions on sewing and fanning seams.

Now it is time to join the four-patch units to the 2½″ strips of white. This is the same process you used when making *Four-Patch Lattice* in Class 240 (page 48). With the 2½″ white strip facing up, position a four-patch on top, right sides together. *Always have the blue square of the four-patch at the top right corner.* Stitch the four-patch unit onto the white strip. Leave about ¼″ of strip, and position another four-patch unit, making sure that the blue square is in the top right position.

Continue until you have 84 four-patch units. If you run short of wide strips, cut enough to finish. (This might happen if there is too much space between the four-patch units.)

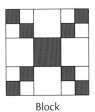

Four-patch units being sewn onto wide strip

Use scissors to cut in the ¼″ space that separates the units. Press the seam toward the white square and starch lightly. Use a ruler and align the seams with the lines of the ruler, and the cut edge of the four-patch. Then, cut the wide strip unit to exactly 2¼″ wide. You will have 84 units, each 4½″ × 2¼″.

The remaining four-patch units will be added to the opposite sides of the white squares to complete Rows 1 and 3 of the block. Check the placement carefully. This time, as you align the four-patch on top of the white square, the white square of the four-patch should be at the top right position. Press the seam toward the white square.

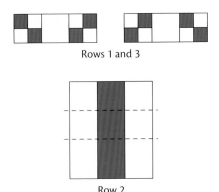

Rows 1 and 3

Row 2

Row 2 is merely three 2½″ strips sewn together—white, blue, white. Sew a blue and a white strip together. Press toward the white; starch and measure for accuracy. Trim if necessary. Add the opposite white strip and repeat the process. Cut into 42 segments, each 2½″ wide. Lay out the units in the order of the block, as shown, and construct the 42 blocks. Fan the seams and press as you go.

Block

Making the Nine-Patch Blocks

The quilt pictured uses a different fabric in each Nine-Patch block. You need to make 30 blocks. If you choose to make yours scrappy like this one, you have a couple of different methods to consider.

One method is to cut 2½″ squares for everything. You will need four 2½″ squares of each of the 30 fabrics and five 2½″ squares of the white for each block. This can be the most efficient use of the fabric—no waste and no extra sewing. Lay out the squares on the sewing table in order. Sew the first two squares of each row together in a chain.

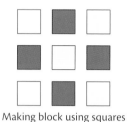

Making block using squares

Press the seam allowances toward the white squares. Add the third square to each row and press toward the white squares. Join the rows and fan the seam allowances as you press. Measure and check that each square along the outside edge measures exactly 2¼″ and that the block is exactly 6½″ square.

A drawback to this method is that if any sewing is not perfectly straight, you won't really know it until the block is constructed.

Another method is to make mini strip sets. Cut the strips a bit longer than needed so you can cut the units using the seamlines as a squaring guide for accuracy. If you choose this method, you will need about 6″–7″ of strip set for Rows 1 and 3 and 3″–4″ of strip set for Row 2. Quarter-yard cuts of fabric work perfectly for this method, as they are 9″ wide, and the strips can be cut along the selvage edge with no waste. Fat quarters can also be used, but not as efficiently.

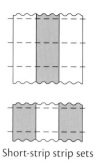

Short-strip strip sets

We are going to let you make this decision. Or you can try both methods and choose your most successful one.

Setting triangles

SIDE-SETTING TRIANGLES

To figure the size of squares needed for the side-setting triangles, work through the formula again. The blocks are 6″ finished:

6″ × 1.414 = 8.48″, or 8.5″ + 3″ = 11.5″

You need 22 side-setting triangles. You get four triangles per square; 22 ÷ 4 = 6 squares needed. Cut 2 strips 11½″ wide. You will get three squares from each strip. Cut these squares diagonally in both directions.

CORNER TRIANGLES

The corner triangles come from squares that are 2″ larger than the finished block; 6″ + 2 = 8″. You need two 8″ squares. These can be cut from the remaining length of the strips used for the 11½″ squares.

Lay out the blocks on your design wall or on the floor. Position the side-setting triangles at the end of the rows and start to sew the rows together. Press the seam allowances of Row 1 toward the setting triangles. From there on, you will be pressing all the seam allowances toward the Nine-Patch blocks.

Once all the rows are constructed and pressed, join the rows to make two halves of the quilt top; then join the halves. Add the corner triangles last.

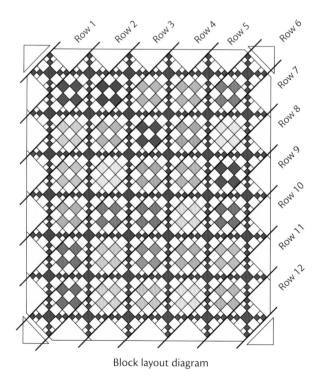

Block layout diagram

If you choose to add borders to this quilt, follow the guidelines in Class 280 (page 96).

Class 260

Our customers at the store are constantly telling us that if they buy one more yard of fabric, their spouses will go off the deep end. Quilters continually justify their fabric purchases. We believe that we quilters need to reassess our thinking and give ourselves permission to be involved in an art that requires working materials. A fabric collection is no different from a stamp collection, or a collection of woodworking tools or golf clubs, for that matter. To be inspired and have the ease of working through our design ideas, it is important that we surround ourselves with fabric. Besides, in quiltmaking, a complete palette of fabric is a necessary tool. You cannot rely on your local quilt shop or Internet sites to have the colors you need when you want them.

LESSON ONE:
Collecting and storing fabric
COLLECTING FABRIC

If you have already started to collect fabric, now is the time to get that fabric organized so you will know what you have. And if you are just starting a collection as you make the quilts in this series of books, you will find it very handy to start cataloging and sorting your fabric now as part of your quilting routine.

The easiest way to organize is by color. So, start by sorting greens, blues, reds, and so forth, into stacks.

Color stacks

Next, arrange all the fabric within each color range by value, from lightest to darkest. If you start to notice big gaps in your light-to-dark group, concentrate on collecting within those areas on your next trip to the quilt shop. If your fabrics flow from light to dark in an unbroken chain, you probably have a nice balance of all values of that color.

Color piles sorted by value

If you really want to get down to the nitty-gritty, you can subdivide these color runs and groupings into stacks based on their intensity. You would have the following stacks:

* Soft, dull colors
* Dark, dull colors
* Soft, bright colors
* Strong, bright colors
* Any other combination that makes sense to you

Once you have done all this, you might begin to see that you have more fabrics of one color, as well as one value and intensity, than the others. We tend to buy our favorite colors over and over, and most quilters purchase more medium values than any other.

If your stacks are looking a bit flat or dull, you are probably missing the "zingers," as quilters call them. Zingers are the "hot," bright, or more intense colors that we often shy away from. Fuchsia, hot pink, yellow, lime, and turquoise are some of these sparklers. On the other hand, if you have only these wild colors, you may need to calm things down a bit with some softer, duller fabrics.

note **Blender fabrics** *Don't overlook your stack of blender fabrics. These are the neutral-colored fabrics that can get lost in a stack of prints. Refer to Volume 1, Class 160 (page 67).*

If you tend to be a very neat, organized person (or if you aspire to be!), this period when you are in the sorting and stacking mood is a great time to start thinking about cataloging your fabrics. This can be as simple as gluing a swatch of every one of your fabrics into a notebook by color. Or it can be as elaborate as making a 3″ × 5″ index card that records as much information as you have about each fabric, including whether you have prewashed it. Once you start to see what you have (or don't have), you will need to go shopping.… Darn!

When you are at the quilt shop, concentrate on collecting by value, intensity, and print scale, not just by color. In future volumes, we will talk more about organizing and cataloging your stash fabrics to make your shopping trips easier and more fun!

Cataloging ideas for your fabric stash

FABRIC STORAGE IDEAS

Whether you are buying fabric quilt by quilt and have leftovers that you want to save or you are building a stash, you will want to devise a storage system for your fabric. Your sewing room situation is an important factor in determining how you store your fabric and how *much* you can store. If you have never organized your fabric or don't have a dedicated sewing space, you may want to experiment with different systems. Stores such as Ikea and The Container Store are all about storage and using space

efficiently. If you have one of these stores, or a similar one in your area, go browse and see what ideas you can come up with.

Fabric storage is very much a matter of personal taste and available space. If you are severely limited on space, small clear plastic storage containers from a home improvement or discount store work very well; you can stash them in a closet, in a basement corner, under the bed, or on a small shelving unit. If you cannot see the fabric colors clearly through the plastic, you may want to label each bin as to what it contains. This will save time when you are looking for fabric for your next project. Avoid storing fabric on unfinished wood or particleboard shelves, because the acids from the wood can discolor and weaken the fabric. (Avoid this problem by painting or finishing the wood with polyurethane or by lining the shelves with aluminum foil.) You might also consider putting glass doors over the front of your fabric shelves or attaching a blind or curtain that you can close when you are not working. These preventative measures will keep dust and light from affecting your collection over time.

Another storage idea is to use a small file cabinet in which you can store your fabric on end, like file folders. When you open the drawer, you can see the top edge of every piece of fabric. This makes it easy to find the one you are looking for and to remove it without messing up the rest of the fabrics in the drawer.

Fabric stored in a file cabinet

LESSON TWO:
Choosing fabrics for sashings and borders

Sashings and borders act as frames around the blocks and the entire quilt. These fabrics need to enhance your quilt, not detract from it.

Think about the following ideas when planning your sashings and borders:

❋ Because of their position and purpose, the color of the border and/or sashing fabrics can influence the color scheme of the entire quilt. The color used for the sashing or the border can be the same color as found in the blocks, or it can introduce a whole new color that enhances the quilt's overall effect. Repeating a predominant color combined with adding one or two new colors can give striking results. Fabrics such as solids and stripes are especially interesting in borders and sashings.

❋ Using a large-scale print that contains the colors of the fabrics in the quilt top can have a dramatic effect and can pull all the colors together, unifying the quilt top, borders, and/or sashings.

❋ Border stripes create a coordinated look to the overall quilt. When mitering corners, the border becomes an elaborate frame, but with very little effort.

❋ Consider how you want to quilt the borders. Remember that a busy printed fabric can be your friend by hiding stitching issues, but it will not let the quilting design show. A solid or small-print fabric allows the quilting to be a focal point, but it will not do much to hide any quilting issues you may still be working out. With practice comes excellence, and you may find that challenging yourself to quilting a solid border is a good way to leapfrog your abilities forward.

LESSON THREE:
Bar sets

Bar set quilts are simply vertical rows of blocks alternated with rows of strips or combinations of strips (sashing). The design blocks are all the same size and can be straight or diagonal. If you use a straight set, the blocks are sewn block to block, with no separating pieces between the blocks in the vertical row. As the blocks get more complex, especially when triangles come into play, secondary designs begin to emerge and can make the row of blocks very exciting.

If you use a diagonal set, you need to add setting and corner triangles to make a straight row, just like in the zigzag sets we discuss next.

Bar set quilts are perfect places to use beautiful stripes and fabrics with viny floral prints for the vertical sashing.

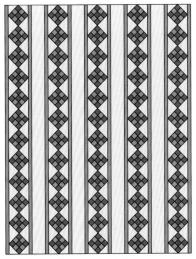

Blocks on-point in bar set

LESSON FOUR:
Zigzag sets

The zigzag set is a very old set for quilts that looks more difficult than it is. This is actually a diagonal version of a strippy quilt. Other names for this setting are Picket Fence and Streak of Lightning. This setting is very distinctive, and most quilts using this arrangement tend to resemble each other more than other settings. The block used in the set becomes the main design element. Try sketching it out on your graph paper, as you will find this to be a helpful guide.

Zigzag set design

This setting requires fewer design blocks to make the complete quilt than most other settings. However, designing it is a bit trickier than standard settings. An odd number of rows are needed to create a symmetrical quilt; an even number of rows does not look balanced. Working with blocks that are larger than 9″ also causes the quilt to become out of balance. Because the blocks read diagonally across the quilt, a diagonal measurement no larger than 12″ is the most pleasing. You also need to

consider working with a block that can be cut in half, as blocks that are not symmetrical might look a bit odd if the half at the bottom of the quilt is different from the half at the top.

Each vertical row of diagonal set design blocks has triangles inserted on each side to create straight sides for the rows. The setting triangles can be cut from solid or print fabric. A print will hide the vertical seams that join the rows, whereas a solid could be a place for beautiful quilting. Undulating quilt designs are beautiful in this space.

The setting triangles are sewn to the blocks, and then the blocks are sewn into rows. In general, all the setting triangles in this set are the same color, but this is not a rule. You might discover a unique look by experimenting with different fabrics or colors.

The side-setting triangles can be made from either method taught in Class 230, Lesson Two (page 24). If you use Method A, the triangles will be an exact fit. We suggest that when the time comes, you try this method and make sure that you have a perfect straight line between the corners of the blocks. If the triangle bows in at all, you would be better off using Method B, which allows room to trim for an exact line.

When constructing the rows, make sure to lay out the blocks in a row and place the setting and corner triangles in their correct positions. Notice on the illustration that the triangles are sitting at opposite angles from side to side. Sew triangles onto both sides of the blocks as you lay them out.

Adding triangles to design blocks

When joining the vertical rows, mark the exact center of the long side of each triangle with a crease or a light pencil mark. This mark will align with the corner of the diagonal block in the adjacent vertical row when the rows are set together.

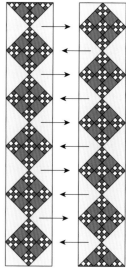

Adding triangles to blocks
and adding center marks

The zigzag setting on the previous page shows how the rows may need a half-block at the top or bottom. This half-block can be either a design or a plain block. Design blocks that have a division at this break work especially well for this set. (Don't forget that a ¼″ seam allowance is needed on the diagonal side if you cut a design block in half.)

Another set design alternates rows that begin and end with full blocks with rows that begin and end with half-blocks.

If you don't care for this style, consider yet another design idea: Construct the rows in the same way, but make the outside triangles into rows and apply the rows as a border. Finish it off by adding the four corner triangles.

Adding another triangle border

The quilts

PROJECT ONE: CARRIE'S *CONFETTI*

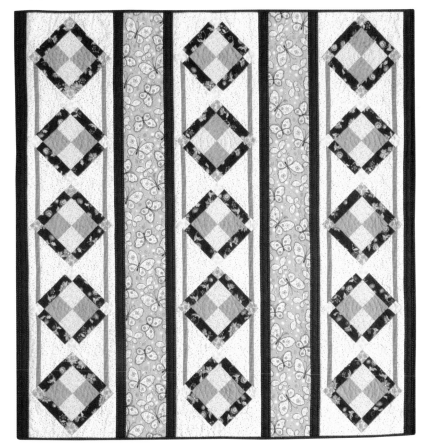

Confetti

Quilt top size: 39½″ × 42½″

Grid size: 1″

Block size: 6″

Blocks: 15

Yardages for quilt top:

⅓ yard green butterfly print

1¼ yards* brown stripe

⅝ yard pink

¾ yard yellow

½ yard brown print

¼ yard medium green

¼ yard light green

1¼ yards cream

⅜ yard** red stripe

Yardage notes

For the brown stripe, you need this much of this fabric only if the fabric you are using is a border stripe that runs the length of the fabric (parallel to the selvage). If you are not using a stripe, you only need ⅓ yard for a quilt this size.

**For the red stripe, again if you are not using a striped fabric, you need ¼ yard of this fabric. If you use a stripe that runs the length of the fabric, first count how many repeats it has from selvage to selvage. If there are more than 24, then you only need the yardage given; if there are fewer than 24, divide 24 by the number of repeats and multiply that number by the 12″ needed to figure your yardage.*

Making the blocks

Formula: 15 blocks, 1 four-patch per block, 2 segments per four-patch = 15 × 2 = 30 segments. The grid for this block is 2″ finished and 2½″ cut:

30 × 2.5″ = 75″ ÷ 42″ = 1.79, or 2 strips

Cut:

2 strips 2½″ wide of both the light and medium greens

1. To start making your pieced blocks, refer to the instructions for the four-patch *Four-Patch Lattice* in Class 240 (page 49).

Completed Four-Patch block

2. Add the brown strips to the sides of your four-patches. The easiest way to do this is to add the blocks to the full strips. Then cut the strips apart and trim them to the size of the four-patch. (This method is similar to what you did for both the *Four-Patch Lattice*, page 48, and the *Four-Patch Chain* quilts, page 70, when you added the wide strips to create the large solid block next to the four-patch. These are just skinny strips.) Press toward the brown strip.

Formula: 15 blocks, 2 strips of brown print per block = 15 × 2 = 30 segments. Measure your four-patch; it should measure 4½″. If it doesn't, use YUM (refer to *Card Trick*, Class 240, page 51).

note *You may want to add an extra ⅛″ to the width of the brown strip so you can trim to make it exact, as we did in* Cabin in the Cotton *(page 43).*

Sewing strip to Four-Patch blocks

30 × 4.5″ = 135″ ÷ 42″ = 3.21, or 4 strips

Cut:

4 strips 1½″ wide of the brown print

Block with brown strips added

3. Construct the top and bottom rows to complete the blocks. Make two different strip sets.

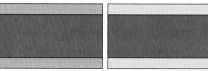

Strip sets A and B

Use YUM for the width of the brown strip, if necessary.

Formula: 15 blocks, 2 strips of brown print per block = 15 × 2 = 30 segments

30 × 1.5″ = 45″ ÷ 42″ = 1.07, or 2 strips (1 strip per colorway)

Cut:

2 strips 4½″ wide of the brown print

Formula: 8 blocks, 2 squares of pink per row, 2 rows per block = 8 × 2 = 16 × 2 = 32 segments

32 × 1.5″ = 48″ ÷ 42″ = 1.14, or 2 strips (1 strip per side)

Cut:

2 strips 1½″ wide of pink

Formula: 7 blocks, 2 squares of yellow per row, 2 rows per block = 7 × 2 = 14 × 2 = 28 segments.

28 × 1.5″ = 42″, or 1 strip

Cut this strip in half so you have one for each side of the brown strip.

Cut:

1 strip 1½″ wide of yellow

Sew your strip sets together and press the seam allowances toward the brown strip, then cut into 1½″ segments.

Lay out the 3 rows of your two different blocks. For all the blocks, sew Rows 1 and 2 together and press toward Row 1. Then add Row 3 and press toward that row.

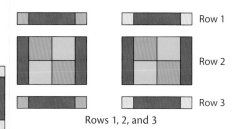

Rows 1, 2, and 3

Adding setting triangles

Now you are going to construct your setting triangles. Refer to the detailed instructions in Class 280 (page 98). Once your setting triangles are made with the stripe in them, you will add them to your blocks. Refer to the diagram.

Add your corner triangles and set these strips aside while you construct the alternate strips of your quilt.

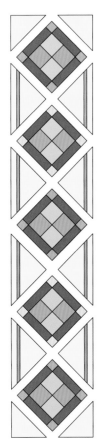

Row assembly for pieced strips of quilt

ALTERNATE STRIP CONSTRUCTION

The middle stripe of this strip is cut 4½″, which is the same width as the four-patches in your pieced blocks. Because this quilt is only 42½″ long, you only need two strips of the green print fabric cut 4½″ wide.

The brown stripes on either side of the green are cut according to the width of the printed stripe of the fabric, which happens to be 1″ finished and 1½″ cut. This measurement mirrors the width of the brown in the blocks. As mentioned under the yardage for this quilt, because this stripe was printed to run the length of the fabric along the selvage, you need enough length to accommodate the length of the quilt without having to piece the stripes together. This means the yardage needs to be at least 42½″.

While you are cutting the four strips needed for this part of the quilt, you can also cut the two strips of brown used as outer borders on the right and left sides of the quilt. Set aside these two strips until you are ready to assemble your quilt top.

Once your strips are cut, piece them together in order, pressing the seam allowance toward the wide strip.

Assembling your quilt top

Now you are ready to assemble the quilt top. Start by sewing Column 1 to Column 2 and Column 4 to Column 5. Then add the two brown borders to Columns 1 and 5. Next add Column 3 to Columns 1 and 2. Finish by sewing the two halves together.

Quilt columns for assembly

PROJECT TWO: HARRIET'S *NAVAJO DREAMS*

Navajo Dreams

Quilt top size: 48″ × 48″

Grid size: 1″

Block size: 6″

Blocks: 30

Yardages for quilt top:

15 – ¼ yard pieces of a variety of prints for blocks

4 yards cream solid for blocks (yes, it is a lot, but correct)

1¾ yards red for setting triangles

We're presenting a new idea with this quilt. This is a reproduction of an old set with an old block. The Album block, also known as Roman Cross, Album Patch, Friendship Chain, and Courthouse Square, has been popular with quilters since the mid-1800s. Let's look at the construction of the block itself.

Traditional Album block

As you can see in the illustration, the block has a diagonal appearance when set straight, but if turned on point it appears straight. Look at the construction of the block. There are numerous pieces and triangles along the edges. Typically, this block would be made with templates, with small triangles along all four edges. Not quite as easy a technique as sewing strips together!

Now let's look at the block differently. What if we wanted to eliminate the triangle templates and that type of piecing, and wanted to work in only strips? It can be done if we sew

accurately and carefully. Examine the illustration below. If all the rows were made into strip units and the ends were cut to create the triangles along the edge, would this block be more appealing to make? There are no diagonal measurements needed, no triangles to work with, and only four different strip sets needed. We will admit that there is quite a bit of waste of the cream background fabric involved in this method, but getting 1″ grid Album blocks by using strips is well worth the waste in our opinion.

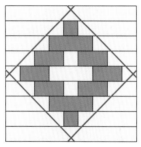

Straight appearance when set on point

We are going to use short strips or fat quarters for the quilt blocks. We have 15 different fabrics that will each be used twice to get our 30 blocks. Each strip set only needs to be 7″–8″ long, so working with ¼-yard cuts is perfect. The strips will be cut on the lengthwise grain and cut 9″ long. If the background fabric is cut into ¼-yard units (9″), then cut into the needed width segments, the cutting will go quickly.

> *note* Be sure to use plenty of starch while constructing these blocks. Once they are cut to size, all edges will be bias and will be sewn onto the bias edge of the side-setting triangle. Starching a bit more heavily than normal will help stabilize these edges and prevent problems from occurring.

Below are the four strip sets needed for each color combination. You will get two blocks from each strip set combination. Rows 1 and 9 are just strips of background.

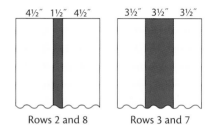

Rows 2 and 8   Rows 3 and 7

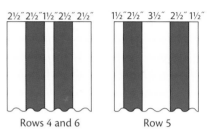

Rows 4 and 6   Row 5

Cut:

Rows 2 and 8:

2 strips background 4½″ wide × 9″ long

1 strip print 1½″ wide × 9″ long

Rows 3 and 7:

2 strips background 3½″ wide × 9″ long

1 strip print 3½″ wide × 9″ long

Rows 4 and 6:

2 strips background 2½″ wide × 9″ long

1 strip background 1½″ wide × 9″ long

2 strips print 2½″ wide × 9″ long

Row 5:

1 strip background 3½″ wide × 9″ long

2 strips background 1½″ wide × 9″ long

2 strips print 2½″ wide × 9″ long

These measurements accommodate enough length to make two blocks from each strip set. Repeat this cutting for the remaining 14 different fabrics.

Construct the strip sets as illustrated on the previous page. We are assuming that you no longer need step-by-step instructions for the basic piecing process. Press all the seams open and starch well.

Once the strip sets are finished, cut the needed segments. Each block needs:

Rows 2 and 8: cut two segments 1½″ long

Rows 3 and 7: cut two segments 1½″ long

Rows 4 and 6: cut two segments 1½″ long

Row 5: cut one segment 1½″ long

Rows 1 and 9: If you have 30 blocks that come from 15 strip sets, you need two segments from each (30 segments total) to accommodate rows 1 and 9. You will need to cut a total of 30 – 1½″ strips of the background fabric. Cut one strip 9″ wide of the cream background fabric. Cut 28 – 1½″ segments from this strip. You need two more 1½″ segments, but you can probably get them from the leftover fabric from constructing the strip sets.

Lay out the segments in the order of the rows shown below in stacks by your machine.

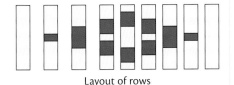

Layout of rows

Sew the rows together, starting with the first two and press the seams open. Be sure to trim after each addition and pressing. Add the third, then the fourth rows, and so on. Continue until all 30 blocks are constructed and pressed. Accuracy is extremely important when constructing the blocks to make sure they can be cut square when finished.

Once the blocks are constructed, it is time to cut them to create 6½″ squares. It is easiest to do the trimming with a ruler that has the ¼″ rule line along all the sides of the ruler. If you have the Side Setting Triangle ruler, the point has these lines and it will do the job fine. Most straight rulers are not as accurate for this type of trimming. There are other rulers on the market that have the ¼″ clearly marked on all sides, and one of these would be a good additional investment.

Position the ruler so that the ¼″ lines are exactly at the seam of the corners of the print strips. You are adding the seam allowance beyond these corners and you need to be extremely careful with the trimming so that when the blocks are cut, they are square and when sewn, the seamline hits the corners exactly.

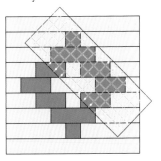

Lay out the blocks on your design wall and position them in a pleasing color pattern. If there is a lot of contrast in the various fabrics, distribute the blocks so that there is a balance. Five of the blocks will extend beyond the top and bottom edge of the layout. These five will be cut in half once the top is constructed.

The next step is to determine the size of the side-setting triangles. Measure the straight side of the Album block. Take that measurement times 1.414. The block will not be an even number—that is okay, as we are not setting it next to anything that has to be the same size. Once you get the measurement of your personal block (ours was a bit less than 6½″) and derive the diagonal measurement (9″), add 2″ to that number. We are not going to make these triangles as large as usual, as there is no need to float anything in this quilt. We need a perfect straight cut line ¼″ from the corners of the block, so we just need enough to trim to an exact straight line. You need 50 side setting triangles.

50 ÷ 4 = 12.5, or 13 squares. If your fabric is 45″, you can get 4 – 11″ squares from each strip, requiring 4 strips 11″ wide. If the selvages are wide or the fabric is narrow, you will get only 3 – 11″ squares from each strip, requiring you to cut 5 strips. Cut the squares the size needed for your blocks (approximately 11″) and cut in half in both directions diagonally.

You need 10 corner triangles. If the blocks are approximately 6½″ square, you will need to cut 5 – 8″ squares, and cut them in half once diagonally.

Once all the setting units are cut, position them on the design wall with the blocks. If there is anything you don't like at this point, this is the time to make changes.

Now you are ready to put the elements together.

Putting it all together

Once the blocks and triangles are in position on the design wall, it is easy to see what has to be sewn together. In a bar set as well as a zigzag set, the columns are constructed first; then the columns are sewn together.

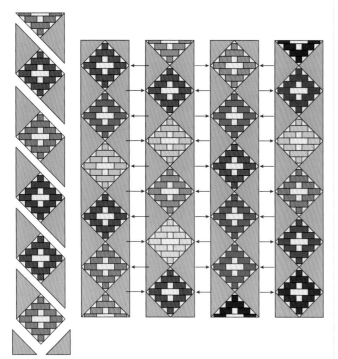

Setting rows together

Start by sewing the side-setting triangles to the opposite sides of the blocks. You will notice that the half-block at the top of column one has one side-setting triangle added to the lower right side. The block at the bottom has two corner triangles on either side. Add the corner triangles after the column is constructed.

Once the columns are constructed, you will need to trim the edges to create a straight line. We did this by placing the 1″ ruler line on the seam of the first square of the Album block. That leaves about ½″ beyond the block point for seam allowance and floating.

Trimming blocks

When sewing the columns together, the exact center of the long side of each triangle needs to be marked with a crease or light pencil mark. This mark then matches the point of the diagonal block in the adjacent vertical row. Pin the first two columns together carefully, aligning the marks and the corners. Sew the first two columns together. Continue in this manner until all the columns are joined.

Once the columns are joined and pressed, it is time to trim the top and bottom of the quilt top. We placed the ruler at the same 1″ mark on the top square of each block to keep the distance the same as the sides.

> *tip* If you find that the blocks are not aligned exactly to cut in half, you might need to add corner triangles to the outside edges of the extended blocks so that when you cut, the background color is attached beyond the point.

> *note* Just to tease your brain, the method used to make the original Card Trick block follows the same idea as Navajo Dreams. Look at the old-style Card Trick block and you will see that it is made of many different triangle units set together in a nine-patch. If that block is turned and redrafted straight, and the new blocks are used in a diagonal setting, you have the same look with a lot less work—and no triangles!

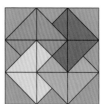

Card Trick—old style

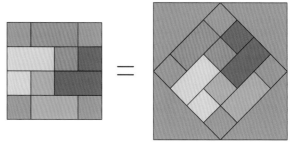

Card Trick—new style

Class 270

LESSON ONE:

Figuring yardage for plain diagonal set quilts

When figuring yardage for diagonal set quilts, a few more steps are involved than for straight-set quilts. We are going to walk you through the process step by step using the photograph of the *Single Irish Chain* quilt top below.

Single Irish Chain, 53″ × 66″

When working off a photograph or drawing, you seldom, if ever, know the size of the block. You are lucky if you even know the size of the quilt! Let's see if we can figure out the size

of the block and the yardage requirements using only a photograph.

We know from the caption that the quilt is 53″ × 66″ finished. Now we need to make some assumptions. Let's assume that each border is 2″ wide finished. That would subtract 6″ off each side, leaving a quilt top 41″ × 54″. What size would the blocks be for this size quilt top?

The blocks are set in a diagonal set, so we need to find the diagonal measurement of the block. If we have 41″ across the top of the quilt and 7 blocks in the row, we need to divide 41″ by 7 to get a rough idea of the diagonal measurement: 41″ ÷ 7 = 5.86″.

Use the chart from Class 230, Lesson Two (page 25), to find the diagonal measurement of various sizes of blocks. The closest measurement to 5.86″ is 5.66″ for a 4″ block: 5.66″ × 7 = 39.62″. This is close to the 41″ needed.

Now let's try for the length of the quilt top: 9 × 5.66″ = 50.94″. Again, this is close to the needed size of 54″.

If we decide that a 4″ block is the needed size, what would the grid be?

4 ÷ 3 (number of grids) = 1.33, which is not a ruler-friendly number.

A 5″ block would give a 49.49″ × 63.63″ quilt, which is too large. It is also not a ruler-friendly size for a Nine-Patch block. Let's split the difference and try a 4½″ block. The diagonal measurement of 4.5″ = 6.36″ × 7 = 44.52″ for the width of the quilt top. This is pretty close to the 41″ we were going for. For the length, the formula would be 6.36″ × 9 = 57.24″. This is also very close to the size we were trying for—and with happy numbers. Finally, a 4½″ Nine-Patch block gives us a grid of 1½″, which is a really nice number to work with.

Now we know the size of the block we are making and the size of the grid.

FIGURING THE YARDAGE FOR THE NINE-PATCH BLOCKS

Count the total number of Nine-Patches in the quilt. There are nine rows of seven blocks: 9 × 7 = 63 blocks. Let's begin by using the formula from Volume 1, Class 170 (page 81).

There are 63 blocks. Each block has 5 blue units (like units). Each unit will need 2″ from a strip to accommodate its position:

$5 \times 2'' = 10''$ of blue fabric needed for each block

63 blocks $\times$ 10″ = 630″ running inches of strips

Each strip is 42″ long.

630″ ÷ 42″ = 15 strips cut 2″ wide

So far, we need **30″ of blue** fabric.

There are 4 white units per block, and each is cut 2″:

$4 \times 2'' = 8'' \times 63 = 504'' \div 42'' = 12$ strips of white cut 2″ wide

We need **24″ of white** fabric.

FIGURING THE YARDAGE FOR THE ALTERNATE BLOCKS

The alternate blocks are solid squares of white. There are 8 rows of 6 squares, which means we need 48 – 4½″ squares. Because these are solid squares, they need to be cut 5″ square (from the Nine-Patch blocks: $3 \times 1\frac{1}{2}'' = 4\frac{1}{2}'' + \frac{1}{2}''$ seam allowance = 5″).

48 squares × 5″ cut = 240″ ÷ 42″ = 5.71, or 6 strips of white cut 5″ wide

We need **30″ of white** fabric.

SIDE-SETTING TRIANGLES

There are eight setting triangles on each side and six on the top and bottom, which means we need 28 setting triangles. We can get four triangles from each square; 28 ÷ 4 = 7 squares. The size of each square to cut in half diagonally in both directions is the diagonal measurement of the block:

4.5″ × 1.414 = 6.36″ + 3″ = 9.36″, or 9½″ squares × 7 squares = 66.5″ ÷ 42″ = 1.58 = 2 strips 9½″ wide

We need **19″ of white** fabric.

CORNER TRIANGLES

We need two squares 4½″ + 2″ = 6½″. We will have 13″ leftover from one of the strips from the side-setting triangles, which is enough to cut the two corner squares.

Now it's time to add up the totals. We have only one number for the blue: 30″.

If we add all the answers for the white, we find that we need 24″ + 30″ + 19″ = 73″ of white, which is just a bit over 2 yards.

Thus, without borders, we would need about 1 yard of blue and 2⅛ yards of white.

BORDERS

If we use the 4½″ block, the quilt top will finish to approximately 44½″ × 57¼″. We strongly suggest making an illustration on a sheet of paper when figuring yardage for borders. Adding length and width plus border width allotments can get very confusing unless you keep the numbers straight on paper.

We are going to stay with the original assumption of 2″ borders. That means we will figure the strips needed based on a 2½″ strip. We need to figure for crosswise-cut strips. Remember that the side borders are added first; the top and bottom borders are last.

We need two strips 2½″ wide by 57¼″ long. Adding these two borders to the sides makes the width of the quilt 48½″ + ½″ for seam allowances, or 49″. Thus we need two strips 49″ long for the top and bottom.

57.25″ + 57.25″ + 49″ + 49″ = 212.5″ ÷ 42″ = 5.06, or 6 strips cut 2½″ wide

We need **15″ of blue** fabric.

Now the quilt top is 61¾″ long by 49″ wide. The side borders are cut 61¾″. The top and bottom borders will need to be cut 49″ + 2¼″ + 2¼″ = 53½″.

61.75″ + 61.75″ + 53.5″ + 53.5″ = 230.5″ ÷ 42″ = 5.49, or 6 strips cut 2½″ wide

We need **15″ of white** fabric.

Now for the last border. The quilt top is now 66¼″ long and 58″ wide.

66.25″ + 66.25″ + 58″ + 58″ = 248.5″ ÷ 42″ = 5.92, or 6 strips cut 2½″ wide

We need **15″ of blue** fabric.

Now add all the numbers together for the borders:

Blue: 15″ + 15″ = 30″ for the borders. If we add the 30″ for the blocks, we get a total of 60″ ÷ 36″ (yard) = 1.67, or 1⅔ yards of blue fabric.

White: 15″ for the border + 24″ + 30″ + 19″ = 88″ ÷ 36 = 2.44″, or 2½ yards of white. Add any extra for errors in cutting and straightening the grain.

These are the minimum amounts that you need.

The finished size of the quilt is 58″ × 71″. Not bad for working off a photograph. We hope you are starting to see how easy this is. You can make any quilt any size with any size block and know exactly how many strips to cut, how many strip sets to make, and how much fabric to buy. Not bad for a few minutes with a calculator.

LESSON TWO: Figuring yardage for diagonal set quilts with sashing

If your quilt has sashing, you will need to add this step to what we did previously. You will need to figure how many block-sized sashes you need to sew between the quilt blocks in each row and on each end. In the example, count up the number of short sashing strips you need.

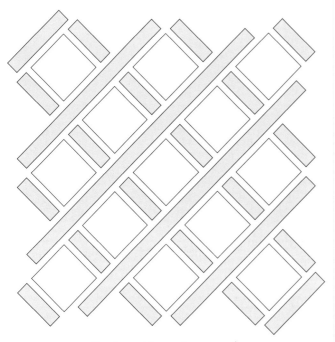

Figuring sashing yardage example

Did you come up with 18? If not, count again. This quilt needs 18 short sashing strips.

Let's say the blocks of this quilt are 7″ finished. That means you need 18 sashing strips 7½″ long: 18 × 7½″ = 135″. Divide this by 42″ to get 3.21, or 4 strips.

Now let's say your sashing is going to be 1½″ wide finished or 2″ cut: 4 strips × 2″ = 8″ of fabric for your block-sized sashing.

Next, look at the long sashing between the rows. Use this two-step math formula for figuring the yardage:

(Finished block size × number of blocks) + (finished sashing size × number of sashes) + ½″

This is easy for the first sashing row, as it is on top of a single block.

7″ × 1 = (7″) + (1.5″ × 2) = 10″ + ½″ = 10.5″

For the next row, you have three blocks and four block-sized sashing strips:

3 × 7″ = (21″) + (1.5″ × 4) = 27″ + ½″ = 27½″

And for the third row, you have five blocks and six sashing strips:

5 × 7″ = (35″) + (1.5″ × 6) = 44″ + ½″ = 44½″

Now, if you count again, you will see that there are two 10½″ strips, two 27½″ strips, and two 44½″ strips.

You now have three options. You can cross your fingers and toes and hope that your fabric is exactly 45″ or maybe even a little wider and that the white part of the selvage is miniscule so that it is wide enough to get those two 44½″ strips out.

Or you can cut your sashing strips on the lengthwise grain of the fabric. The latter option will give you a lot of left-over fabric, but it will make getting those two long strips easier.

If you choose to do the strips without piecing, then you need a length of fabric long enough to accommodate the 44½″ length—1¼ yards, though for safety, you may want to round that up to 1⅓ yards.

You can always piece the strips, but this is one solid piece of fabric, and the seam would likely show. Even if the fabric is a print, the seam will probably show up. If that doesn't bother you, then add up the total running inches you need and cut all your strips from 42″-wide fabric. For this example, you would need 4 strips cut 2″ wide, or ¼ yard of fabric. Two of the strips would be subcut to give you the 27½″ pieces and the 10½″ pieces; the extra would be used to make the long 44½″ strips pieced together. Make your decision based on your fabric choice and your preferences, and figure your yardage accordingly.

LESSON THREE: Designing with internal frames

As you progress further into quiltmaking, you will probably start to get tired of the same old strips sewn around the edge of your quilt tops to make borders. Perhaps a pieced block in the corners adds a bit of spice, but overall the borders get boring. What if you could add some excitement within the quilt top by piecing frames into the blocks and setting triangles of the diagonal set?

Internal Frames is our name for a concept that Mary Ellen Hopkins created in the early 1980s called Incorporated Borders. Harriet was at Mary Ellen's Summer Camp seminar in the summer of 1985 when Mary Ellen first introduced the concept. It was the buzz of the seminar and was one of Mary Ellen's greatest ideas—one that is worthy of visiting again. She never published her idea, but she shared many designs with the students in that seminar. The assignment was for each student to design as many incorporated borders as he or she could dream up. Needless to say, Harriet has a notebook of ideas that were freely shared that summer.

These designs have also been referred to as *Painless Borders* and *Built-In Borders* by Sally Schneider. We have changed the name because we do not see them as borders so much as a frame that is then bordered by the setting triangles and by even more strip borders beyond that.

Traditional pieced borders can really add a great deal of design impact to a pieced or appliquéd quilt top. The problem gets to be the math involved in drafting them and getting the units to fit the quilt top perfectly. As you have learned, what the calculator says, what you cut and sew, and what you actually get can be very different numbers in reality. To plan a complex pieced border and have it actually fit properly is asking a lot, especially from a beginner. Mary Ellen's concept was to design a border into the actual "on-point" blocks of the diagonal set. Her theory was based on making the elements of the border designs into blocks and setting all the blocks of the quilt diagonally, ending up with a quilt with a complex pieced border (frame), without the hassle of math and complex piecing.

There are a few guidelines to get you started with these frames. First, try to keep the blocks easy to construct. For now, the pieces used in the frame design should be squares or rectangles. (In Volume 3, we will introduce using triangles in these frames.) The simplest designs will fit blocks made from a nine-patch, four-patch (16-square unit), or five-patch (25-square unit) grid.

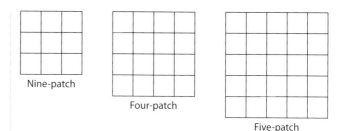

Nine-patch, four-patch, and five-patch design units

To start with, design the center of the quilt top. Use any block that you can position on-point. The blocks can be large or small, but remember that the frame blocks will be created from the same size block as is used in the center of the quilt top.

Refer back to Class 250 (page 64) to plan the size of quilt you want to make. Decide on a setting style and block size. Are you using alternate plain blocks, linking blocks, or two different pieced blocks?

Once you have your blocks pieced, go to your design wall and lay out the blocks. Then count the number of blocks needed for the side frames, the corners, the side-setting triangles, and the corner triangles. The illustration on the next page shows the placement of these blocks. You have 18 design blocks. You will need 10 side frame blocks and 4 corner frame blocks, 14 side-setting triangles, and 4 corner triangles. Can you locate and identify all of these blocks?

> *note* Sally Schneider was also introduced to the idea in one of Mary Ellen's seminars. Once she bought a computer and design software in 1986, she started playing with the idea, first by doing Ohio Stars and then on to ideas of changing parts of the border blocks, and got big and little squares. One idea led to another and before she knew it, she had many borders— turning them into three books in the end. Sally says: "I think this is what's called simultaneous discovery—and it happens a lot." If you are interested in Sally's books, two of which are out of print (Painless Borders and Traditional Quilts with Painless Borders), check on used-book websites under her name and you will find them. The third book, Designing with Built-In Borders, is still in print and available from Sally. Check the resources page at the end of the book for information. Sally's books are full of designs, from simple to fairly complex, and will inspire you to explore these design ideas even further.

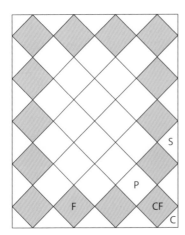

How many pattern (P) blocks? _____

How many frame (F) blocks? _____

How many corner frame (CF) blocks? _____

How many side-setting (S) triangles? _____

How many corner (C) triangles? _____

Here are two more illustrations of different-sized quilt tops to think about when designing your quilt. These are just a few of the dimensions you can work with when designing your own quilt top. Try 3 × 4, 3 × 5, and 5 × 6. Refer to the chart in Class 250, Lesson Two (page 64), for quilt dimensions based on the size of the design block and the layout you have chosen.

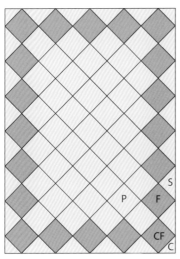

5 × 7 blocks

How many pattern (P) blocks? _____

How many frame (F) blocks? _____

How many corner frame (CF) blocks? _____

How many side-setting (S) triangles? _____

How many corner (C) triangles? _____

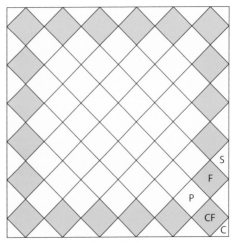

6 × 6 blocks

How many pattern (P) blocks? _____

How many frame (F) blocks? _____

How many corner frame (CF) blocks? _____

How many side-setting (S) triangles? _____

How many corner (C) triangles? _____

Now you can begin to design the internal frame. Start by looking at how these frames develop. The first illustration uses Nine-Patch blocks that place a dark square in the center of the block, surrounded by light squares. Notice how the construction of these blocks achieves the desired effect.

Simple frame using Nine-Patch blocks

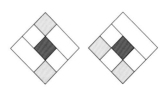

A slightly more complex frame uses small four-patch units within a Four-Patch block. By placing the darker fabric in the small four-patch squares, a continual line runs around the body of the quilt top, framing the center of the piece. The color chosen for the setting triangles and in the frame squares gives the appearance of a border. Notice the change in construction of the blocks for the corners.

Five-Patch block using a chain of small squares

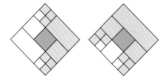

Four-Patch block using large and small squares

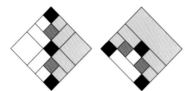

More complex design with four-patch units

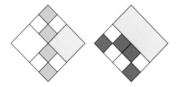

The following designs are from worksheets given out in the *It's Okay if You Sit on My Quilt* Summer Camp seminars in 1985. Most are Mary Ellen's designs, but some were designed in class by the students. Because their names were not on all the copies, we owe an apology for not giving credit to anyone who might deserve it.

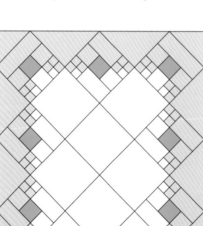

Nine-Patch block using large and small squares

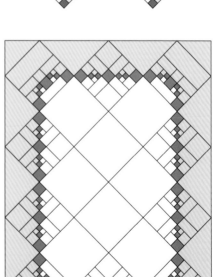

Five-Patch block using large and small squares

Have fun with these! This is fun graph paper work. Start by designing the center of your quilt top, then choose a frame; or choose the frame first and design the blocks for the center afterward. Don't forget that color changes really affect the appearance. The outside half of the frame block, the setting triangles, and the corners can all be totally different colors. Or the frame can float by using the same background color in the entire frame block and setting triangles, then add more color by adding strip borders onto the setting triangles. The possibilities are endless!

DRAFTING INTERNAL FRAMES

Internal frames, also known as incorporated borders, are a row of pieced blocks added all the way around the quilt, forming an internal border or frame around the design blocks. We have already explained how to design these frames; there really isn't any magic to it. Once you have your design blocks drawn out on diagonal set graph paper, draw one or two rows of blocks to surround the design blocks. Then start to play. You may find that some quilts look best with the frame right up next to the blocks or as an extension of the blocks. Other quilts may look best with the frame separated from the design blocks by a row of plain blocks.

When designing and drafting your own internal frames, keep in mind that the frames will generally work best and look most pleasing to the eye if you mimic or mirror the elements, or at least the scale of elements, that are part of the design block(s).

We suggest that you spend some time playing with these ideas by drafting out a few of your favorite blocks, set on-point, and then adding different internal frames. Have fun!

PROJECT ONE: *STAR CHAIN*

Star Chain

Star Chain is our first quilt that introduces internal frame blocks. This simple block uses combined grids and measuring for YUMs. All the blocks are the same, so the instructions will give you the formulas for how many strips to cut and the strip sets needed. We are not going to give detailed sewing instructions, as we hope that by now you have that down.

Quilt top size: 46¼″ × 52½″ (includes borders)

Grid size: 1″

Block size: 4¼″

Blocks:

20 design blocks

30 alternate blocks

18 frame blocks

4 frame corners

Yardages for quilt top:

1½ yards blue

5 yards brown

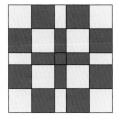

Design block

Let's break this block into units and come up with the strip set formula so you have a recipe for constructing this block.

Rows 1 and 5

This unit represents the strip order for the strip set. There are 2 units in each block and 20 blocks.

2 × 1.5″ (cut size) = 3″ × 20 = 60″ ÷ 42″ = 1.43, or 2 strip sets needed

Cut:

4 strips 1½″ wide of blue

4 strips 1½″ wide of brown

2 strips 1″ wide of blue

Sew all four 1½″ blue strips to the 1½″ brown strips, making four pairs. Press toward the brown. Check each strip for accuracy (1¼″ from seam to raw edge) and trim if necessary. Add a 1″ strip of blue to two of the strip sets. Press toward the brown strip and measure. Be really careful with this little strip. It needs to finish at ½″. Add the remaining pair of strips to the 1″ blue strip. Press toward the brown. Measure the strip set width; it should measure exactly 5″.

> *tip* Because the 1″ strip is so small and needs to be an accurate ½″ finished, you might want to cut the strips 1⅛″ instead of 1″. This will let you trim the strips after the first side is sewn on to keep it straight and more accurate.

Cut the strip sets into 40 segments 1½″ wide.

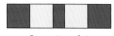

Rows 2 and 4

The formula is the same for rows 1 and 5, but the colors are reversed.

Cut:

4 strips 1½″ wide of brown

4 strips 1½″ wide of blue

2 strips 1″ wide of brown

Repeat the sewing steps, remembering to reverse the colors. Refer to the illustrations to keep the order of the strips straight.

Row 3

This row is different from the rest, and it relies on the YUM method of measuring.

The strip that fills the center position is a combined grid unit. It must measure exactly the same as the three center units of the other rows. Do you remember doing this for *Double Irish Chain* and *Inlaid Tiles* in Volume 1 (page 84)? Turn over one unit from Row 2 and measure from the raw edge of the seam allowance to the raw edge of the seam allowance of the three center units. This is your YUM. If you are really watching your accuracy, it should measure exactly, or very close to 3″. This will be the width you need to cut the center brown strip.

There is only 1 unit per block × 20 blocks = 20 × 1″ = 20″ = 1 strip set.

Cut:

2 strips 1½″ wide of blue

1 strip 3″ wide (or YUM) of brown

Once all the units are constructed, press the seams toward the brown, cut 20 segments, and make stacks of 20 units for each row. Chain sew the first two rows together. Fan the seams if you desire, though this is not necessary. Press and starch. Continue adding rows until the 20 blocks are constructed.

Alternate block

The quilt top has 30 alternate blocks that are cut the same size as the Star Chain blocks (5″ unfinished). When cutting solid blocks, it is easiest to figure the number of strips it will take by dividing the length of the strip by the size of the block: $42″ ÷ 5″ = 8.4$. Thus, you will be able to get 8 blocks per strip. $30 ÷ 8 = 4$ strips are needed to get 30 alternate blocks.

Once these are cut, you might want to put the blocks on your design wall to see how they are coming together.

Next, we will build the internal frame blocks.

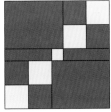

Internal frame side block

The internal frame block has three different units. The first is a four-patch.

Four-patch unit

Referring to the illustration on page 92, count the number of internal frame blocks. How many blocks do we need? 18, right? There are 2 four-patches in each block, and each four-patch has two segments. Each segment is cut 1½″ wide.

$4 × 1½″ = 6″ × 18 = 108″ ÷ 42″ = 2.57$, or 3 strip sets

Cut:

> 3 strips 1½″ wide of brown
>
> 3 strips 1½″ wide of blue

Sew the strips together into pairs. Press toward the brown strip. Measure for accuracy. Construct 36 four-patch units. Fan the seams and press.

Plain brown unit

The four-patch units will be sewn onto plain units of brown.

$2 × 2.5″ = 5″ × 18 = 90″ ÷ 42″ = 2.14$, or 3 strips cut 3″ wide

Cut 36 units 3½″ wide from these strips. Add a four-patch unit to one end of each. Press toward the brown unit.

Center strip

$1 × 1″ = 1″ × 18 = 18″ ÷ 42″ = 0.43$, or 1 strip set

Cut:

> 1 strip 3″ wide of brown, cut in half lengthwise
>
> 1 strip 1″ wide of blue, cut in half lengthwise

Sew the strips together, taking care to keep the 1″ strip straight and accurate. The center strip needs to measure ½″ after pressing. Cut 18 segments 1″ wide.

All the units are now constructed and ready to turn into blocks. Make stacks of 18 units for each row to form a block. Sew the rows together, fanning the seams and pressing after

each addition. These blocks need to measure exactly 5″ square. How are you doing?

Framed corner block

Although you only need four frame corner blocks, they are a bit complex. You might be able to cut some of the units from leftover strips.

First unit

2 units × 1½″ = 3″ × 4 blocks = 12″

Cut:

> 1 strip 1½″ wide of blue, then cut in half lengthwise
>
> ½ strip 1″ wide of brown

Sew the strips together and press toward the brown strip. Cut 8 segments 1½″ wide from the strip set.

Brown spacer

This brown spacer can come from leftovers—either a wide strip or a narrow one. Here is the formula for cutting a narrow strip that will be cut into 3″-long units:

3″ × 4 = 12″ strip cut 1″ wide

Cut:

> ½ strip 1″ wide of brown, subcut into 4 – 3″ strips

Sew the two units together to create the center of the block. You will get four centers.

Brown sides

Next, add the two sides to the block centers.

2 × 3″ = 6″ × 4 = 24″ = 1 strip cut 1″ wide

Cut this strip into 8 segments each 3″ long. Attach these to the sides of the center units.

Final unit

This is from a single strip:

5″ (the width of the unit) × 4 = 20″

Cut:

1 strip 1½″ wide of brown; then cut 4 – 5″ long strips

Attach this to the top of the center unit.

Single strip

The final unit will be made from leftovers, as you don't need enough to make a strip set.

Cut:

8 – 1½″ squares of blue

4 pieces 1½″ × 4¼″ of brown

Sew blue squares onto the ends of the brown pieces. Press toward the brown unit. Attach this to the bottom of the block.

Add these internal frame blocks to your design wall. The last thing to do before you start constructing the quilt top is to figure the side- and corner-setting triangles. Count the number of each you need on the quilt layout illustration.

Side setting triangles

The unfinished block is 5″ square:

5″ × 1.414 = 7.07″ + 3″ = 10″ cut squares

22 triangles are needed for the edges:

22 ÷ 4 = 6 squares needed

42″ ÷ 10″ = 4 squares per strip

22 ÷ 4 = 6 strips

Cut:

6 – 10″ wide strips of brown; then cut these squares in half diagonally in both directions. Position the triangles on the design wall.

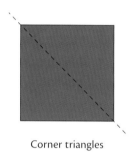

Corner triangles

The block is 5″ square + 2″ = 7″ for corner triangles. You need two 7″ squares. Cut these in half diagonally. Save them until all the rows are joined together. The corners are the last units to go on the quilt top.

Join the blocks into rows and join the rows together. When you are ready to apply the borders, read Class 280 (page 96) first. The borders on this quilt are 1″ wide finished for the blue stripe and 3″ wide finished for the brown.

Star Chain layout

PROJECT TWO:
4'S AND 9'S WITH
INTERNAL FRAME

This quilt has six different blocks that all consist of the same elements but in different configurations within each block. We will walk you through determining the number of strips you will need for each block. We refer you to previous quilts for the actual sewing techniques if you still need some guidance for the actual sewing processes.

Quilt top size:

68″ × 68″ (with borders)

Grid size: 1″

Block size: 6″

Blocks:

13 of Block A

12 of Block B

36 solid alternate blocks

12 of frame block A

8 of frame block B

4 frame corners

Yardages for quilt top:

3 yards white

1 yard light teal

1 yard teal print

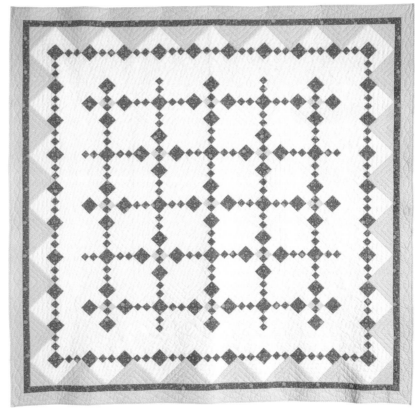

4's and 9's with Internal Frame

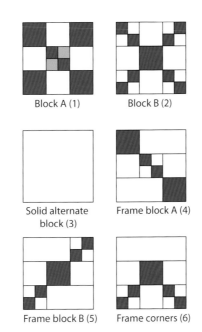

Block A (1)   Block B (2)

Solid alternate block (3)   Frame block A (4)

Frame block B (5)   Frame corners (6)

The six blocks that make up this quilt

The first three blocks are in the interior of the quilt; the last three make up the internal frame. Start by adding up all the four-patch units needed for all the blocks; make them all at one time for efficiency. Then you can address each element individually.

Two-color four-patch unit

Block 1 has a two-color four-patch unit. There are 13 blocks. The four-patch is a 1″ grid and uses two segments from the same strip set for each unit.

2 × 1.5″ = 3″ × 13 blocks = 39″ = 1 strip set needed to make 26 segments

Cut:

1 strip 1½″ wide of light teal

1 strip 1½″ wide of teal print

Teal and white four-patch unit

This unit is used in Blocks 2, 4, 5, and 6.

Block 2 = 4 units per block × 12 blocks = 48 units

Block 4 = 1 unit per block × 12 blocks = 12 units

Block 5 = 2 units per block × 8 blocks = 16 units

Block 6 = 2 units per blocks × 4 blocks = 8 units

Total units needed from strip set = 84 four-patch units

2 segments per unit × 1.5″ = 3″ × 84 = 252″ ÷ 42″ = 6 strip sets

Cut:

   6 strips 1½″ wide of white

   6 strips 1½″ wide of teal print

Construct four-patch units as taught in Class 240, Project 2 (page 49), or in Volume 1, Class 150 (page 56).

When you look at all the blocks, notice that Blocks 2, 5, and 6 all have the above element. We can make them all at once for efficiency.

Block 2 = 1 unit per block × 12 blocks = 12 units

Block 5 = 1 unit per block × 8 blocks = 8 units

Block 6 = 1 unit per block × 4 blocks = 4 units

Total number of units from strip set = 24 units

24 units × 2.5″ (cut segment length) = 60″ ÷ 42″ = 1.43, or 2 strip sets needed

Cut:

   4 strips 2½″ wide of white

   2 strips 2½″ wide of teal print

Construct the strip sets and cut into 24 segments 2½″ wide.

Block 1 has two segments of this unit per block.

2 × 2.5″ = 5″ × 13 blocks = 65″ ÷ 42″ = 1.55, or 2 strip sets

Cut:

   4 strips 2½″ wide of teal print

   2 strips 2½″ wide of white

Construct the strip sets and cut into 26 segments 2½″ wide.

Block 4 has two segments of this unit per block.

2 × 2.5″ = 5″ × 12 blocks = 60″ ÷ 42″ = 1.43, or 2 strip sets

Cut:

   2 strips 4½″ wide of white

   2 strips 2½″ wide of teal print

Construct the strip sets and cut into 24 segments 2½″ wide.

Blocks 2 and 6 have this unit. How many white strips do we need to connect the four-patches to?

Block 2: 2 segments × 2½″ = 5″ × 12 blocks = 60″

Block 6: 1 segment × 2½″ = 2.5″ × 4 blocks = 10″

70″ ÷ 42″ = 1.67, or 2 strips

Cut:

   2 strips 2½″ wide of white, subcut into 28 – 2½″ squares

Construct the units as explained in *Four-Patch Chain*, Class 250 (page 71).

Block 5 has two of these units per block.

2 × 2.5″ = 5″ × 8 blocks = 42″ ÷ 0.95″ = 1.19, or 1 strip

Cut:

   1 strip 4½″ wide of white, subcut into 16 – 2½″ × 4½″ units

Sew 16 four-patch units to these strips.

Blocks 1 and 4 need white squares, but how many? Each block has one unit each with two white squares in each unit.

2 × 2.5″ = 5″ × 25 (total number of both blocks) = 125″ ÷ 42″ = 2.98, or 3 strips

Cut:

   3 strips 2½″ wide of white, subcut into 50 – 2½″ squares

Block 6 has one segment of this strip.

1 × 2.5″ = 2.5″ × 4 blocks = 10″

Cut:

   1 strip 6½″ wide of white, subcut into 4 – 2½″ × 6½″ units

Block 3 is a solid square of white. There are 36 in the quilt top.

36 × 6.5″ = 234″ ÷ 42″ = 5.57, or 6 strips needed

Cut:

6 strips 6½″ wide of white; then cut into 36 – 6½″ squares

Note: The 2½″ segments needed for Block 6 can be cut from the ends of these strips once the 6½″ squares are cut.

You now have all the elements needed to construct all the blocks. Using these segments, lay out all the blocks in stacks and construct. Double-check the direction you pressed the seam allowances to make sure all the seams will butt.

Once all the blocks are constructed, pressed, and checked for squareness and accuracy (they should all be exactly 6½″ square), it is time to go to the design wall to lay out the blocks, using the illustration for guidance.

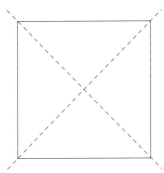

The last elements to work through are the side- and corner-setting triangles.

Side triangles:

Add up the total number of side-setting triangles. Six per side:

6 × 4 sides = 24
24 ÷ 4 (triangles per square) = 6 squares
Block size: 6″ × 1.414 = 8.48″ = 8.5″ + 3″ = 11½″

Cut:

2 strips 11½″ wide of light teal; then cut 3 squares from each strip. Cut each square diagonally in both directions.

Corner triangles:

6″ block + 2″ = 8″ squares (2 needed)

Cut:

1 strip 8″ wide of teal print

Cut 2 – 8″ squares. Cut in half diagonally.

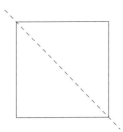

Quilt layout

Position the triangles on the design wall. You are now ready to assemble the rows and join them into a quilt top.

We hope you have enjoyed working through the thought process of constructing blocks by working only from the formulas and drawings. You should be realizing that if you do the designing, figure the yardage, and make up a strip set recipe, you are weaning yourself from having to always use a book or pattern for every quilt you want to make. It truly gets easier as you do it!

Borders:

We added two simple borders to the outside of the quilt top. The first border is from the darker fabric and is 1″ wide finished. The outside border is 3″ wide. The first border is aligned exactly with the block corners. Please read Class 280 (page 96) before cutting and adding borders.

Class 280

LESSON ONE:

Squaring a diagonal set quilt top

Squaring up a diagonal set quilt is a bit different from working with a straight set quilt. In Volume 1, we showed you how to fold the quilt in half to check that the sides were the same length and the top and bottom were the same width. In that case, you could easily make adjustments within the seam allowances to correct any deviations.

Diagonal sets present a different set of concerns. Because everything is diagonal (on the bias), the method of measuring used in Volume 1 does not work. Instead, you need to work off the points of the blocks that are along the sides of the quilt top. It would be great if you could just measure out from the points and cut off any excess fabric that is not wanted along the edge! Unfortunately, it's not quite that simple.

Once the quilt top is finished and the final pressing is done, it is time to find a large flat surface that will allow you to measure across the width and/or length of the quilt top. You also need to decide how much of the side-setting triangles are going to extend beyond the corners of the blocks; Do you want the binding to butt right up against the points, or do you want to float the triangles out beyond the corners?

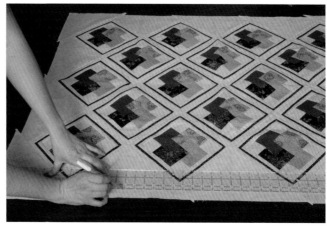

Ending with triangles right at corners of blocks

1. Measure the desired distance from each block corner and make a mark. Do this on all four sides of the quilt top.

Measuring from block corners

2. Measure across the width of the quilt top. You are trying to establish one width measurement that will be consistent down the length of the top. Measure from one mark across the quilt top to the opposite side. Note the measurement. Continue doing this at every mark across the quilt. If all the measurements are the same, it is your lucky day! Unfortunately, that is not generally the case. You will probably see a bit of a difference from one pair of marks to the next. The goal is to establish the same width down the quilt sides by adjusting the marks to be further out or closer in where needed. The marks will not all be the same distance from the block corners; this is only a problem if you are planning to finish the binding right up to the corners. If you want to float the blocks, this adjustment will be barely noticeable.

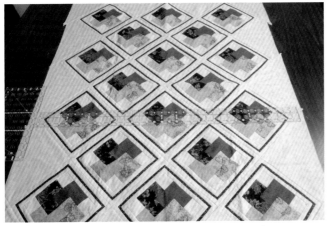

Measuring across the top from mark to mark

3. Repeat Step 2 for the length of the quilt top by measuring from end to end and checking the measurement at each mark. Adjust and remark as necessary.

4. Use a long straightedge to join the marks into a straight line. Be sure that the marker you are using will completely come out of the fabric, as you are marking the seamline for a border or for the binding.

Joining the marks for a straight edge

5. Use a large square ruler to square the four corners. Align the ends of the right angle with the lines you just established—both the top and side of one corner. Once these lines are connected, check within the ruler to make sure that the ruler lines are squared and aligned with the interior piecing of the blocks and setting triangles.

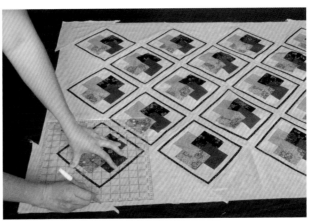

Squaring the corners

6. Once everything is square, draw a line to connect the corner with the sides. Repeat for all four corners. Next, measure out ¼″ and draw another line. This will be the cutting line—*but don't cut the edge yet.* If no borders are going to be added to the edge beyond the setting triangles, you are ready to mark, layer, and quilt the top. Use this excess fabric along the edge as a handle to help you control the edge as you quilt. Once the quilting is finished, the edges can be remeasured and trimmed. Because quilting can cause some contraction and distortion, always remeasure before trimming to bind the quilt.

LESSON TWO:

Sewing the first plain border

If you want to add a border beyond the triangles, the process is very much like you learned in borders for straight sets in Volume 1, Class 180 (page 95). To obtain the length that the border needs to be cut, you need to measure through the center of the quilt top from the top to the bottom marks to arrive at the measurement that the border needs to be cut. Once the border is cut, find the center and mark it; then find the quarter divisions and mark them. Remember to add extra to the ends so that you can square them before adding the top and bottom borders. Make a mark at the ends at the length needed. The bit you added for squaring is beyond these marks.

After you have prepared the borders, position the raw edge of the border against the outside line that you drew previously in Lesson One. Center the border and pin in place. Pin the quarter divisions and the ends in place. You will sew on the border before you trim away the excess fabric of the side-setting triangles. Once you have sewn on two opposite borders, you might want to press the seam toward the border and remeasure across the quilt top to check that the distances are the same along the length of the borders. If there is any deviation, make the correction now.

Once checked, you can trim off the excess setting triangle fabric ¼″ from the seamline. At the ends of these borders, draw a line that extends (on top of the border) the line you drew on the quilt top. Make sure that the corner is square with both the border seam and the drawn line. This line will be the placement line for the next border at the corner. Repeat the process for the top and bottom borders.

> *tip* Remember to cut each border at least ¼″ wider than the correct measurement to allow for trimming once the border is sewn on. You want the border to be exactly the width desired. You also want it to be a straight edge that you can work with when adding the next border. Do not trim if there are no more borders to be added. Once the quilting is finished, you can trim and clean up the edge before binding.

Pieced side and corner triangles

If you find that your quilt lacks pizzazz and the edges just seem to sit there, you might want to consider using pieced side and corner triangles. We had that problem with *Card Trick*. The blocks looked great with the windowpaning, but the quilt top just faded out to nothing in the side-setting triangles. When we added a narrow accent strip of the windowpaning fabric within the side and corner triangles, it perked up the design.

When designing the triangles, you can use either two or three fabrics. The same fabric can be repeated on both sides of the strip, or a different fabric can be used on either side of the strip. At this point, auditioning on the design wall really helps.

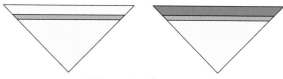

Fabric options for triangles

This is also a wonderful place to position small stripes. There is so much interest in many of the stripes available, but quilters tend to have trouble knowing where to use them. Windowpaning, small borders, and sashing are great places to let stripes shine.

SIDE-SETTING TRIANGLES

Measuring for the side triangles makes great use of the Creative Grids Side Set Triangle Ruler. You can use this see-through ruler to figure how large to make the triangles, as well as where to place the inset strip at the design wall. You will want to do this before you sew the rows together, as these triangles are added as you make the rows.

The ¼″ seam allowance is also marked on the ruler. You might need to make a light mark on one of the blocks at the end of the row to mark the seam allowance. Place the ¼″ ruler line on top of the block's seamline. Use the cross lines of the ruler to determine where you want the strip to be in relation to the corner of the pieced blocks.

Position ruler on design wall

The width of the strip you need for the point of the triangle is the measurement from the ¼″ mark at the point of the ruler to the line where you chose to place the accent strip. Be sure to add ¼″ for a seam allowance allotment to both sides of this strip.

Cut the accent strip to the width that you have decided looks best for your project and color choices.

The outside strip is also measured from the Side Set Triangle Ruler. Position the ruler on the design wall and measure out from the accent strip line to however far you want the triangles to extend and float. Add ½″ seam allowance to this measurement. Now you know what size triangle is needed to fill the position and extend out from the corner of the blocks.

You can also do the planning on graph paper to double-check your measurements. We used 8-to-the-inch graph paper. The strip is 42 squares long, and each square equals 1″. With the graph paper, you can draw in any size triangle and see how many you can get from one strip. You can also see how wide you need the strips to be on either side of the accent strip.

To determine the number of strips it will take to accommodate these triangles, you need to either waste every other triangle from one sized-to-fit strip or make extra-wide strips that will accommodate cutting from both sides. If you only cut from one side, you will need to measure the outside length of the triangle and multiply it by the number of triangles you need. For example, let's say you need a cut triangle that has a long side measurement of 14″. You will be cutting strips from 42″ fabric, from which you can get three triangles: 42″ ÷ 14″ = 3. You need 10 side-setting triangles. Because 10 ÷ 3 = 3.33, you will need 4 strips to get the total number of triangles. This method leaves quite a bit of waste, but it is easier to figure out the sizes of strips to sew together.

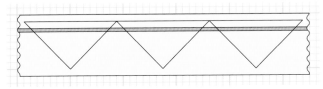

Cutting from one side of strip

If you decide to make a wider strip to cut from both sides, it isn't difficult to do, especially when using graph paper. The diagram shown here shows that you can get five triangle units from one strip by making it wider.

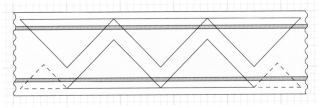

Cutting from both sides of strip

Because each square on the graph paper equals 1″, you just need to count the squares to know the size of each strip. Draw in the triangles and then count the squares. In the first example, the strips are 2 squares (one extra for the margin at the edge), ½ square, and 6½ squares (one extra for the margin at the edge). We added one square to both outside edges, so that makes the cut strips 2½″, 1″, and 7″. Don't forget to add seam allowances (½″) to each side of each strip and to the long edge of the triangle.

The second example works the same way. We diagrammed the strip set and drew in the triangles, so we know we have plenty of height to get opposing triangles in the center. The strips count out to be 2 squares, ½ square, 7 squares, ½ square, and 2 squares. The extra square on each outside edge has been added, as have seam allowances. Thus, the strips would be 2½″, 1″, 7½″, 1″, and 2½″.

Sometimes when using sashing, the corner block is not actually square; it is wider than it is tall. This affects the size of the side and corner triangles. You might find that the accent strip looks best when it is centered exactly in the center of the side triangle. If that is the case, it is very easy to prepare the strips for cutting: You only need three strips, and they are the same width on both sides of the accent strip. As an example, let's go back to the size triangle used above. The long side is 14″, which means the height of the triangle is 7″. If you place the accent strip right in the center, it is 3″ from each side. Now the triangle can be cut side by side without an offset. Add a bit extra beyond the cut edges of the triangle on the width of the fabric strips.

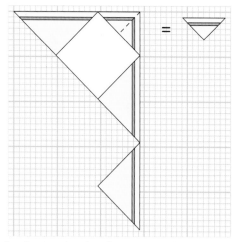

Graph paper drawing of setting triangles and corner

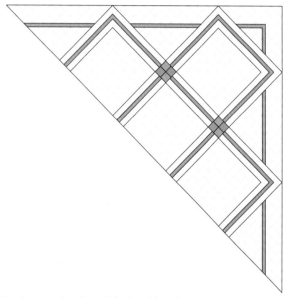

Graph paper drawing of blocks with sashing and setting triangles

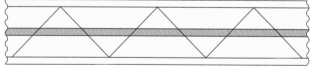

Cutting side by side

CORNER TRIANGLES

Drafting the corner on graph paper really helps you determine the strip width needed and the position of the accent stripe. The corner triangles are much smaller than the side triangles, and the stripe is closer to the inside corner.

Diagram of corner

Determine the sizes of strips you need to cut to get these triangles.

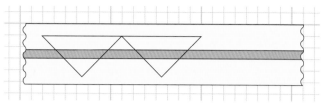

Strips for corner triangles

Counting the grids, you find that the long side of the triangle is 7″. If you are careful when placing the large triangles on the strips you made for them, you can likely get two corner triangles out of the waste at the end of the strips. You need two triangles for each corner. If you need to make a separate strip, count out the squares again: 2 squares, ½ square, and 2½ squares would result in a strip 2½″, 1″, and 3″.

Piece two of these triangles together to create the turned corner. Repeat three times to yield four corners. Carefully match the intersections so that the narrow stripe turns the corner accurately. Press the seam open.

> *tip* You might find it more exact and easier to make a template the size you need your triangle to be, with the accent stripe drawn on it for placement. A template allows you to double-check the size and position at the design wall before constructing the strip sets.

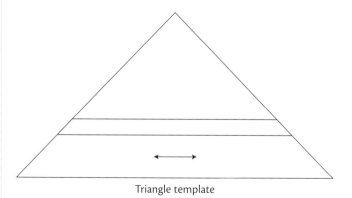

Triangle template

This was a bit of work, but well worth it for what these triangles add to the edge of the border. Congratulations for trying!

Class 290

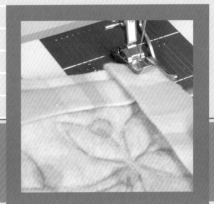

LESSON ONE:
More binding options

In your freshman year (Volume 1), we covered choosing quilt backings, squaring the corners, and straightening the quilt edges in preparation for applying the binding. We also covered one method of basic binding, how to join the ends of the binding strips on the bias, and finishing the binding ends. In this volume, we cover an optional way to join the ends of the strips, especially if you found the cut ends difficult to keep accurate. In this lesson, you will learn another way to join the ends after sewing the binding on, which will look like all the other seams, making it very difficult to find where you started and stopped.

REVIEW
PREPARING THE QUILT EDGES

Carefully trim all edges of the quilt layers. At the corners, use a large square ruler to make sure that the corners are perfectly square. If the batting is less than ¼″ thick, you can cut the layers all at the same time.

GRAINLINE

When binding a straight-edged quilt, we prefer straight-grain binding over bias binding, as it keeps the quilt edge straight with no ripples. A bias binding is "stretchy" and may give the quilt a stretched appearance along the edge. In addition, the quilt may appear to ripple when hung or placed on a bed. However, a bias binding is recommended for a quilt with rounded corners and scallops.

One argument for bias binding is that the edge of the binding will not wear as badly because there is not a single thread in the weave that runs along the edge (as there is in straight-grain binding). Our argument is for crosswise-cut binding strips, but cut slightly off-grain. Most of the time the grain is off on the bolt. Therefore, when you fold the center-fold to the selvages, the strips are not perfectly on grain, yet they are not true bias. Instead of straightening the grain, leave it off-grain as torn and cut the strips perpendicular to the center fold (crosswise grain). This gives you the best of both methods; the grain is slightly off, allowing more threads to take the wear, but it is not nearly as stretchy as bias.

PREPARE THE BINDING STRIPS

The width of the binding is whatever you think looks best on any particular quilt. Reproduction quilts look best with bindings that are ¼″ wide or smaller, whereas more contemporary quilts might look better with ⅜″ to ½″ binding.

BASIC FORMULA

Cut the binding strips 4 times the desired finished width plus ½″ for seam allowances. Then add ⅛″–¼″ for the thickness of the batting. The fatter the batting, the more you need to allow here.

This formula is just a general guideline. Batting thickness cannot be predetermined or even measured until you have sewn a bit of binding onto the edge and have actually turned it over to the back.

METHOD B:
JOINING THE STRIPS

Your freshman year had you joining the binding strips using a 45° angle at both ends of each strip. The strips were joined by chain sewing the ends into a continuous length (Method A, Volume 1, page 104).

The method presented here for joining the strips will eliminate the need to cut the ends at 45° angles. Instead, make sure that the ends are perfectly squared off.

Position the strips at 90° angles to one another. Stitch from corner to corner, keeping the triangle of the corner on the right side of the needle when stitching. Use a stitch length of 1½ or 2.

Sewing from corner to corner

Open the strip to check for accuracy. The edges of the strips should be perfectly straight on both sides of the seam. Trim the seam allowance to ¼" and press the seam open.

DETERMINING THE CORRECT SEAM ALLOWANCE FOR APPLYING BINDING TO A QUILT

Here is a clever way to determine the actual seam allowance needed for each size of binding:

1. Lay out the binding on the ironing board. Apply a light layer of heavy-duty starch to the wrong side of the binding. Fold the binding in half and press. The starch will help the layers stick together. Press the entire length of the binding strip.

> *tip* For very accurate binding, use a ruler and rotary cutter to measure from the fold. Trim to be exactly the same width the entire length of the binding.

2. Fold the binding in thirds, but leave just a bit less than ⅛" beyond the last fold on the raw edge side. This extended edge is the allowance for the batting thickness.

3. Finger-press the folds. At your sewing machine, position the needle in the fold line of the first fold from the folded edge of the binding.

4. Position a barrier-type seam guide against the folded edge of the binding. This will be the seam allowance with which you will sew the binding onto the quilt.

5. Sew a sample first. Start by stitching about 3" of binding onto the quilt edge. Stop and wrap the binding. The folded edge should just cover the stitching on the back of the quilt. If it is too tight, take a slightly smaller seam; if it is a bit empty, take a slightly wider seam.

Following this method will give you perfect binding every time.

METHOD B: ATTACHING BINDING TO QUILT EDGE

In Volume 1, we joined the ends of the binding on the quilt by sewing down the bottom point and stuffing the finishing end into the pocket created by the sewing at the start. This time, we are going to join the ends with a seam so that this join will look exactly like the seams that joined the strips together.

1. Starting in the middle of one side of the quilt, leave about 8" of binding loose before beginning to stitch. Align the raw edges of the quilt with the binding. Begin stitching the binding onto the quilt edge.

2. At the corner, stop ¼" from both edges of the quilt.

Stop ¼" from corner.

> *tip* Check to see whether the bar in front of your needle on the presser foot measures ¼" or whether there are markings on the side of the foot that measure ¼". Many machines have this feature; this is an excellent way to know when to stop.

3. With the needle down, pivot the quilt and stitch straight backward off the edge of the binding.

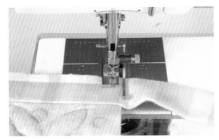

Pivot and stitch backward off the edge.

4. Pull the quilt out from under the foot a bit so that you can work with the corner. The mitered corner is a simple twofold step. First, fold the free end of the binding over the stitched binding to form a 90° corner. The free end of the binding is off the quilt at this point. The diagonal fold in the corner of the binding will be the miter.

Fold binding back to start forming miter.

Second, fold the free end of the binding back onto the quilt. This second fold should line up with the top edge of the quilt. Make sure this fold is a couple of threads beyond the raw edge of the binding underneath.

Bring binding over top to form miter.

5. Start stitching at the edge of the fold. Stitch the binding to this side of the quilt. Repeat for all the corners.

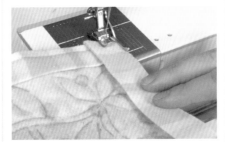

Start stitching at edge.

6. Once the binding has been attached all the way around the quilt, make sure you have left 12″–16″ open. On a flat surface and with the binding opened to a single thickness, pin the ending tail along the quilt edge.

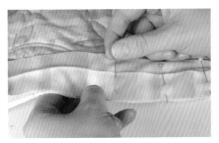

Pin end of binding flat to quilt layers.

7. Make sure that the beginning tail was cut at a 45° angle. Smooth the beginning tail over the ending tail. Following the cut edge of the beginning tail, draw a line on the ending tail with a removable marker. Check that this line is at a true 45° angle to the binding's long edges.

Beginning edge laid over flattened binding; mark.

8. Fold the beginning tail out of the way and add the seam allowance by drawing another line ½″ down from the first line. This second line is the cutting line, so make sure that you are marking and cutting to make the binding ½″ *longer* than the first line.

Add ½″ seam allowance.

9. Cut on the second line.

Cut.

10. Place the ends right sides together and join with a ¼″ seam allowance. Press the seam open. Press this section of binding in half and finish sewing to the edge of the quilt.

Join ends with ¼″ seam allowance.

FINAL STITCHING

Freshman year taught you how to do a blind stitch to secure the binding to the back of the quilt. This lesson will show you the ladder stitch, which is less visible than the blind stitch but is a bit slower.

Use a 40/3 quilting thread for strength and a size 9 or 10 sharp or appliqué needle. (Appliqué needles are more slender and longer than sharps.)

1. Knot your thread and then run the needle through a part of the seam allowance. Bring the needle into the fold of the binding. Go directly below this exit point of the needle into the batting and backing, just below the stitching line. Take a ¼″ stitch and pull the thread through the fabric.

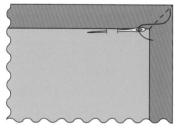

Stitch in batting and backing only.

2. Position the point of the needle directly above where it came out of the fabric and insert it into the fold of the binding. Take a ¼″ stitch and pull the thread through.

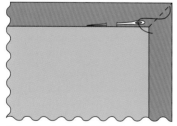

Second, stitch in fold of binding only.

3. The stitch is ¼″ in the fold, then ¼″ in the backing/batting, then ¼″ in the fold again. The stitches are straight down; there is no slant to them as with blind stitching.

Ladder stitch

4. Repeat until you get to a corner. At the corner, stitch down each side of the miter with a very small stitch. Stitch to the end of the miter, push the needle through to the front side, and continue back down the front side of the miter. Once you get back to the inside corner, push the needle through to the back side and continue down the binding with the longer stitch.

Tip: As you stitch, tighten the thread a bit every inch or so by pulling it gently. The stitches will disappear in the fabric.

We hope you enjoy this second method of binding. If you had any problems following the illustrations last time, we hope the photographs make the methods more clear.

LESSON TWO:
Quilting designs

As you become increasingly interested in quiltmaking, you will want to start studying the actual quilting on quilts. You will probably start to find that the quilting plays a big part in the beauty of the final product. Below are some things you can start to search out and collect to get ready for the amazing quilts you will be making by the end of this series.

✳ Start a clipping file to store any pictures of quilts and quilting designs that you find in decorating magazines.

✳ When you go to quilt shows, take close-up photos of quilt designs that you like. A digital camera with the flash turned off will really show quilting texture.

✳ Carry a sketchpad when traveling. Architectural details such as Victorian moldings, iron fences, gates, and tile work can all inspire quilting and piecing designs.

✳ Look at old china, greeting cards, coloring books, holiday decorations, and wallpaper for ideas.

✳ Take some time to visit the Dover Publications website to see the amazing array of copyright-free books they have. These books are filled with wonderful ideas.

We have once again illustrated the way we quilted the quilts in this book. Notice that the quilting is becoming progressively more detailed. Carrie is the driving force behind the quilting designs, as she is learning to quilt while we are making the quilts for these books. Once in a while, Harriet needs something a bit more challenging; so if you think the quilting is too difficult, that is why. As this series continues, the quilts will become more difficult and the quilting more intricate. If you are learning to quilt as you work through these classes, you will see your quilting skills improve along with your piecing. It is our hope that you learn both together so that you are ready to make fantastic quilts by Volume 6. Harriet's book *Heirloom Machine Quilting* is an excellent workbook to have beside you each step of the way.

This is just another step of your adventure into the quilting aspect of quiltmaking. Always remember that it is not a quilt until it is quilted.

Nine-Patch on Point

Cabin in the Cotton

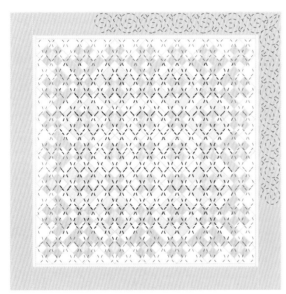

Metro Main Street

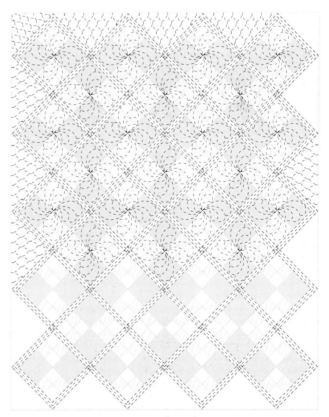

Four-Patch Lattice

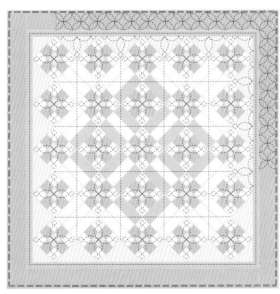

Irish Garden

Card Trick

Four-Patch Chain

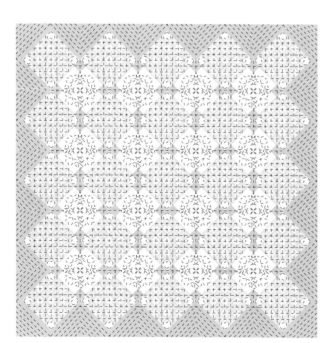

Five-Patch Chain

Confetti

Navajo Dreams

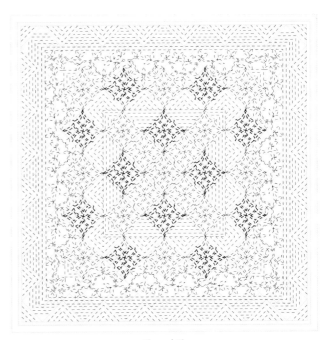

4's and 9's

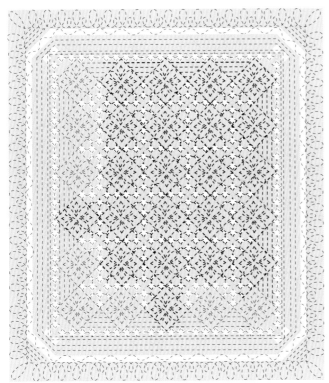

Star Chain

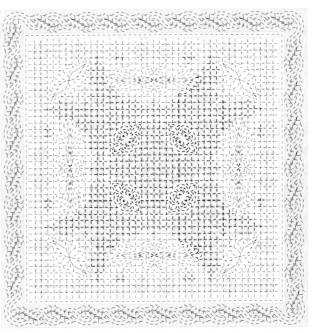

Ice Crystals

Your Sophomore Final

Okay, you have completed another set of lessons and projects, and you should be comfortable with diagonal sets. The original quilt that Carrie has designed is meant to take you one step further in your ability to understand grid size, identify units and strip sets, figure yardage, and create a recipe for quilts made of just strips and squares set on the diagonal.

Here you will find a picture of *Ice Crystals,* a variation of *Burgoyne Surrounded.* This quilt was chosen for your sophomore final because it incorporates everything you have learned from both Volume 1 and Volume 2.

As in Volume 1, there are no construction or assembly instructions for this quilt. We have provided you with a worksheet so you can do your own calculations, choose your own grid, figure the yardage needed, and make your own strip set recipe.

As a hint, you may want to start by redrafting the block illustration on graph paper, breaking the block units apart like we did in the final for Volume 1. Also, note that we did not include the side-setting triangles for this quilt. It is up to you to decide whether you would like to finish your quilt as Carrie did or you would like to have the borders finish differently.

Enjoy the process and have fun!

Ice Crystals

ICE CRYSTAL WORKSHEET

Block Unit 1

How many Unit 1's are in one block?

_____

How many are needed for all five blocks? _____

How many inches of strip sets are needed to accommodate the number of units needed? _____

Block Unit 2

How many Unit 2's are in one block?

_____

How many are needed for all five blocks? _____

How many inches of strip sets are needed to accommodate the number of units needed? _____

Block Unit 3

How many Unit 3's are in one block?

_____

How many are needed for all five blocks? _____

How many inches of strip sets are needed to accommodate the number of units needed? _____

Block Unit 4

How many Unit 4's are in one block?

_____

How many are needed for all five blocks? _____

How many inches of strip sets are needed to accommodate the number of units needed? _____

Sashing Unit 1

How many Sashing Unit 1's are in one block? _____

How many are needed for all five blocks? _____

How many inches of strip sets are needed to accommodate the number of units needed? _____

Sashing Unit 2

How many Sashing Unit 2's are in one block? _____

How many are needed for all five blocks? _____

How many inches of strip sets are needed to accommodate the number of units needed? _____

Framing Block Units

Side Frame Block Unit 1

How many Side Frame Block Unit 1's are in one block? _____

How many are needed for all four blocks? _____

How many inches of strip sets are needed to accommodate the number of units needed? _____

Ice Crystals block

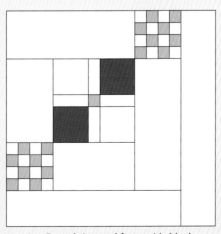

Ice Crystals internal frame side block

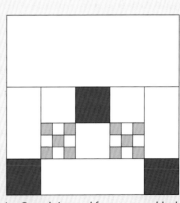

Ice Crystals internal frame corner block

Side Frame Block Unit 2

How many Side Frame Block Unit 2's are in one block? _____

How many are needed for all four blocks? _____

How many inches of strip sets are needed to accommodate the number of units needed? _____

Side Frame Block Unit 3

How many Side Frame Block Unit 3's are in one block? _____

How many are needed for all four blocks? _____

How many inches of strip sets are needed to accommodate the number of units needed? _____

Side Frame Block Unit 4

How many Side Frame Block Unit 4's are in one block? _____

How many are needed for all four blocks? _____

How many inches of strip sets are needed to accommodate the number of units needed? _____

Side Frame Block Unit 5

How many Side Frame Block Unit 5's are in one block? _____

How many are needed for all four blocks? _____

How many inches of strip sets are needed to accommodate the number of units needed? _____

Side Frame Block Unit 6

How many Side Frame Block Unit 6's are in one block? _____

How many are needed for all four blocks? _____

How many inches of strip sets are needed to accommodate the number of units needed? _____

Corner Block Units

Corner Frame Block Unit 1

How many Corner Frame Block Unit 1's are in one block? _____

How many are needed for all four blocks? _____

How many inches of strip sets are needed to accommodate the number of units needed? _____

Corner Frame Block Unit 2

How many Corner Frame Block Unit 2's are in one block? _____

How many are needed for all four blocks? _____

How many inches of strip sets are needed to accommodate the number of units needed? _____

Corner Frame Block Unit 3

How many Corner Frame Block Unit 3's are in one block? _____

How many are needed for all four blocks? _____

How many inches of strip sets are needed to accommodate the number of units needed? _____

Corner Frame Block Unit 4

How many Corner Frame Block Unit 4's are in one block? _____

How many are needed for all four blocks? _____

How many inches of strip sets are needed to accommodate the number of units needed? _____

Corner Frame Block Unit 5

How many Corner Frame Block Unit 5's are in one block? _____

How many are needed for all four blocks? _____

How many inches of strip sets are needed to accommodate the number of units needed? _____

Corner Frame Block Unit 6

How many Corner Frame Block Unit 6's are in one block? _____

How many are needed for all four blocks? _____

How many inches of strip sets are needed to accommodate the number of units needed? _____

About the authors

Harriet started quilting seriously in 1974, working alongside her mom. Her early quilting career included producing baby quilts for craft shows and teaching adult education classes. In 1981, Harriet opened her quilt shop, Harriet's Treadle Arts. Her specialties at the time were free-motion embroidery, machine arts, and machine quilting.

In 1982, Harriet attended one of Mary Ellen Hopkins's seminars. Mary Ellen's streamlined techniques and innovative design ideas led Harriet to a new way of thinking, which caused her to give up the machine arts and to teach only quilting. Today, she is world renowned for being a true "mover and shaker" in the quilt world. In the late 1990s, she was voted one of the "88 Leaders of the Quilt World."

Harriet created and inspired a whole new generation of machine quilters with her best-selling book *Heirloom Machine Quilting,* which has enjoyed 22 continuous years in print. She is also the author of *Mastering Machine Appliqué* and *From Fiber to Fabric,* and co-author of *The Art of Classic Quiltmaking.* She is responsible for a myriad of products pertaining to machine quilting, and she has developed batting with Hobbs Bonded Fibers and designed fabric for P&B Textiles.

Carrie has been around quilting all her life—sitting in Harriet's lap as a baby while Harriet sewed, learning her colors with machine embroidery thread and her alphabet on the cams of Harriet's old Viking sewing machine. She didn't have a chance not to be involved! Harriet and her mother opened the store when Carrie was four years old, and she spent a part of nearly every day of her life at the store. Carrie's interests in college turned to range management and wildlife biology, but no matter what, she always came home to quilting as a hobby.

In 2006, Harriet decided she wanted to close the store. She was tired after running it for 25 years as well as traveling and teaching at the same time. Carrie couldn't imagine not having the store as a part of her life. So she moved back to Colorado and now runs the store full-time.

Most of all, Carrie is proud to carry on the family legacy of quilting that extends from her great-great-grandmother Phoebie Frazier, to her great-grandmother Harriet Carey, to her grandmother Harriet (Fran) Frazier, to her mom, Harriet. Quilting is all about tradition (no matter how you make a quilt) and about the love of creating something beautiful from fabric and thread with your own hands.

All the quilts in the book were pieced and quilted by Harriet and Carrie. They truly believe that if you are going to teach it, you had better be able to make it!

Resources

SUPPLIES/SOURCE LIST

All notions and supplies referred
to in the text are available from

Harriet's Treadle Arts
6390 West 44th Avenue
Wheat Ridge, CO 80033
303-424-2742
www.harriethargrave.com

Information on Harriet's classes, retreats, and
conferences can be found on her website.

Sally Schneider
Sally Schneider Quilts
1.4.8 Calle Chulita NW
Albuquerque, NM 87114
www.sallyschneider.com

If you are looking for copies of Harriet's out-of-print books
referred to in the text, they are available through C&T
Publishing as e-books. *From Fiber to Fabric* is also available in a
print-on-demand edition. Go to www.ctpub.com to purchase.

Other titles by Harriet Hargrave:

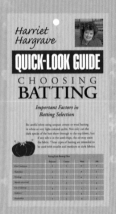